At HIAS, the Jewish community's global refugee agency, we describe the evolution of our mission as going from helping refugees because they were Jewish to helping refugees because we are Jewish. In *Three Groundbreaking Jewish Feminists: Pursuing Social Justice*, Dr. Sharon Leder takes us into the lives of three inspiring women, all leaders in human rights and social justice, and explores how their being Jewish influenced their own journeys for justice. This book should be reading for anyone – male or female, Jewish or gentile – interested in making a difference while on this planet and in making that difference with empathy.
Mark Hetfield, President and CEO of HIAS,
The Global Jewish Refugee Agency

A profound meditation on the meaning of Judaism, social justice, and identity politics in the twentieth century, through the extraordinary lives of three Jewish women activists-- Gerda Lerner, Susana Wald, and Ruth W. Messinger. Through their passionate, courageous, and creative journeys defined by the horrors of War World II and the arrival of Hitler to power, the reader is invited to explore the vicissitudes of history. This is a most exceptional and original book on the power of the human spirit to resist adversity. A memorable read impossible to put down.
Marjorie Agosín, Professor of Spanish, Wellesley College.
Author *A Cross and A Star: Memoir of A Jewish Girl in Chile*, and *Always From Somewhere Else: A Memoir of My Chilean Jewish Father.*

In a time of fragmentation, the breakdown of society and culture as we know it, Sharon Leder gives us a roadmap for healing. *Three Groundbreaking Jewish Feminists* gives us courage and hope that we can join three brilliant visionary women who, by their example and work, have influenced our time toward a better world. By choosing to write about women who devoted their lives to causes larger than themselves, Dr. Leder documents their identity struggles, their relation to Judaism, their personal suffering, their growth in understanding, and their unwavering belief in and contribution to social justice. It is a must-read.
Kathleen Spivack, Visiting Professor Emerita, Université de Paris,
École Polytechnique. Author *Robert Lowell and His Circle: Plath, Sexton, Bishop, Rich, Kunitz et al*, and the novel *Unspeakable Things.*

Can one be committed to Jewish particularism—concerned with Jewish well-being and survival—as well as to universalist values of justice and equality for all peoples? In this fascinating study of three exemplary Jewish feminists, two of whom are Holocaust survivors, Sharon Leder explores how each woman wrestles with this question. Each one draws on her particular experience and professional field–history, art, and international relations–to arrive at a commitment to humanitarian service.

Robert Melson, Professor Emeritus Political Science,
Purdue University. Author *Revolution and Genocide: On the Origins of the Armenian Genocide and the Holocaust,* and a memoir, *False Papers: Deception and Survival in the Holocaust.*

Sharon Leder powerfully and insightfully tells the stories of three very different Jewish women—scholar Gerda Lerner, artist Susana Wald, and activist Ruth Messinger—and, with scholarly depth and illuminating anecdotes, demonstrates how each was inspired by her Jewish identity to adopt a universalistic vision and to make the world better for others. Leder demonstrates that—as per Ruth Messinger's favorite classical Jewish quotation—these three strong Jewish women knew it was not incumbent upon them to complete the work of healing the world, but their Jewish backgrounds impelled them to do what they could. Leder, whose own personal story also fits this pattern, helps us to be similarly inspired.

Rabbi Robert Scheinberg, Ph.D.,
rabbi of United Synagogue of Hoboken, NJ

Three Groundbreaking Jewish Feminists Pursuing Social Justice offers a well-researched analysis of the complementary yet sometimes tension-inducing interactions between Judaism, Jewishness, and feminism. Throughout this honest and self-reflective account, Leder interlaces her thoughts about literature, art history, and religion and provides a vigorous portrayal of the effects of feminism on the spiritual and secular lives of three Jewish women. Indeed, the strongest feature of the book is its refreshing new way of exploring how particular peoples' experiences may be universalized for a larger conversation about social justice, Judaism, and feminism in the women's studies community.

Tonia St. Germain, JD, retired Director of Women's and
Gender Studies, Eastern Oregon University. Co-editor, with
Susan Dewey, of *Conflict-Related Sexual Violence: International Law, Local Responses,* and co-author, with Susan Dewey, of *Women of the Street: How the Criminal Justice-Social Services Alliance Fails Women in Prostitution*

Sharon Leder's book is a welcome contribution to the movement of Jewish spiritual renewal. As a Rabbinic Chaplain I often hear Jewish people say that they are not sure about the existence of God, but they believe in good deeds and kindness as the way to heal the world. The lives of Gerda Lerner, Susana Wald, and Ruth W. Messinger demonstrate universal values as pathways to peace, values that transcend boundaries of color, class, gender, sexual identity, and nation. This book is a valuable and fascinating read for people of all religions and no religion. It leaves me grateful for the lives of these women and the ways they changed our world.

Shulamit Fagan, Founder ALEPH
Jewish Renewal Rabbinic Pastor Program

Sharon Leder has given us a significant work, long sorely needed. In *3 Groundbreaking Jewish Feminists: Pursuing Social Justice* she traces the rich and complex lives of three ordinary/extraordinary Jewish women to demonstrate the nuance, precarity, and strength of Jewish lives and possibilities. With a feminist focus navigating the thorny relationship between universals and particulars, we learn about each woman and a wealth of Jewish history, struggle, and potential.

Marla Brettschneider, Professor Women's and Gender Studies/
Political Science, University of New Hampshire.
Author *Jewish Feminism and Intersectionality.*

Dr. Sharon Leder in this book has given us a steadfast, loving testimony about three feminist Jewish women working for justice for all God's children, no matter what! This witness is rooted in the particularity of Judaism made manifest in seeking to stand with the oppressed, the poor, and the marginalized. The repair of the world. It brings to my mind the words of 'Mother' Pollard, an elderly black woman who after participating in the Montgomery bus boycott for many weeks said, "My feets is tired but my soul is rested."

Fr. Ken Campbell, Episcopal priest and longtime convener of the
Nauset Interfaith Association, Cape Cod, Massachusetts

Three Groundbreaking Jewish Feminists: Pursuing Social Justice shows two sides of humanity, one of persistent infliction of pain and damage to human life throughout history and the other of resilience on the part of survivors who fight back for justice and peace. Lerner's and Wald's narratives exemplify the suffering of millions of Jews under the Nazi regimes which swept Europe during War II as well as the lives of those dedicated to upholding ethical, moral principles of Judaism to help other people. Messinger, from pluralistic,

multi-cultural New York City, advanced the plight of the poor and minorities of different colors and faiths being guided by her conviction that social justice and equality are universal norms among all religions. Dr. Leder's book articulates issues of faith and secularism in the contemporary world and makes a valuable contribution to understanding common bonds among different religions.
Abdul H. Raoof, Professor Emeritus,
Political Science, SUNY-Buffalo State

This notable book introduces us to three diverse and impressive women, grounded in their Jewish identity, whose universal ideals led them to intersect with political realities, not as victims but empowered persons. Sharon Leder has given us an important work, meticulously researched, clear, concise and beautifully written. As a retired Methodist minister of the United Methodist Church, I am indebted to the author for expanding my understanding and appreciation of these remarkable women and the social justice tradition in Judaism they represent.
Rev. Dr. Kent Moorehead, Orleans, MA

Dr. Sharon Leder has given us insight into three gifted Jewish women who, through their own Jewish journeys, lead the reader on differing paths to 'Tikkun Olam' *(Repair of the World)*. Dr. Leder makes us understand that although the roots of our Judaism are diverse, it is possible that we are all intertwined with the history and commandments of our Torah. Powerful and insightful! I would recommend this book to anyone who is interested in the question of what makes a strong woman a strong *Jewish* woman.
Cantor Pamela Siskin, Cantor Emerita,
Congregation Beth Israel, West Hartford, CT

Three Groundbreaking Jewish Feminists

Pursuing Social Justice

SHARON LEDER

HybridGlobal
PUBLISHING

Published by
Hybrid Global Publishing
301 E 57th Street
4th Floor
New York, NY 10022

All quotations from the Hebrew Bible from *Tanakh: A New Translation of The Holy Scriptures According to the Traditional Hebrew Text*, The Jewish Publication Society, 1985.

Manufactured in the United States of America, or in the United Kingdom when distributed elsewhere.

Leder, Sharon
Three Groundbreaking Jewish Feminists: Pursuing Social Justice
LCCN: 2020924538

ISBN: 978-1-951943-42-4
eBook: 978-1-951943-43-1

Cover design by: Jonathan Pleska
Copyediting by: Claudia Volkman
Interior design by: Suba Murugan
Author photo by: Michael Krassner
Cover: Detail from *Maremoto* (Tsunami) and
    interior illustrations by Susana Wald
Index by: Larry Baker

www.sharonleder.com

CONTENTS

FOREWORD

In her exceptionally insightful book, Sharon Leder presents an interesting take on identity politics. Chronicling the lives and words of three prominent yet very disparate Jewish women, she reveals the complex intricacies of how we formulate our identities, not only over the life-course, but over socio-historic time as well. Covering different stages of these women's political identities, she shows the often ambivalent and complex ways in which we come to know ourselves personally and politically; where, so to speak, the particular and the universal meet in our lives. Each woman's life-path brings into focus the ways in which our multiple identities merge and re-emerge, dominate and recede, in the making of our personal and political understandings of the world and our place in it.

By illuminating the complex relationships between and among their personal and political selves, as professionals, women, and Jews, Sharon Leder presents them as forerunners to the contemporary debates about intersectionality, post-Holocaust Jewish identities, and contemporary variations on Jewish identity. She uncovers the variety of relationships Jews often have with their Jewishness, religious, ethnic, and/or secular. That variety includes even those who might fall into a newly defined category, as is found in the 2013 PEW Research Report, which uses the category JNR (Jewish Not by Religion) to reflect the self-identification of 22 percent of contemporary American Jews.

Jonathan Rauch's review of Mark Lilla's *The Once and Future Liberal: After Identity Politics* asserts that the most powerful force for social movement change in the twentieth century was identity politics. After all, he reasons, he was able to marry a same-sex partner only after homosexuality became an identity, a normatively recognized way of being in the world.

Now, however, Rauch believes we should move beyond identity politics toward an articulation of that which we commonly share. But perhaps this needs some rethinking.

In his new book, *Modernity and the Jews in Western Social Thought*, Chad Alan Goldberg argues that Jews have served as a significant reference in debates about what it means to be modern. Social theorists, argues Goldberg, invoke differences between Jews and non-Jews to reflect and create key binaries within contemporary social thought. The focus on difference from the other, real or fictive, in the past follows us into the present as the "stuff" of modern social thought and identity making. It continues to be how we come to define who we are culturally and politically.

Identity politics makes transparent and visible those groups who have been denied access and/or power as part of the communities and societies of which they are a part. Moving "beyond" identity politics assumes that we no longer have a need for it. But ours is not a utopian world. Economic divisions tied to class, race, ethnicity, religion, and gender/sexuality—to name a few—exist and are always in play as we define ourselves against the "other," not only in theory but also in practice.

One of the most important functions of identity politics has been to make apparent the unequal distribution of resources, material and non-material, in our society and to make visible and transparent the oppressive politics of those who believe they best represent the common good. The politics of identity has made transparent not only the inequities among and between us, but also the power differentials that maintain those differences in the ways we experience our everyday lives as individuals and as communities.

Each woman in this book, in her own way, does just that. Each has given voice to those who have been invisible and/or whose voices have been suppressed. Each of them has used their intersecting identities as Jews, as women and as activists to inform their identity politics toward the "other." Each has used their skills as historian, global humanitarian, and artist to make their politics evident. Through the lives and stories of three women, this book makes evident the complex processes that go into the making of our identity politics. Each reveals her Jewishness as part of her intersecting set of identities: Gerda Lerner declares that she is an historian because of her Jewish experience as both a survivor of the Holocaust, as an antifascist, as an immigrant, and as an unskilled worker; Susana Wald, having converted to Catholicism during the Holocaust, declares herself publicly Jewish in the midst of her activist experiences as part of the 2006 Oaxaca uprisings in Mexico; and Ruth W. Messinger devotes herself to "repair the world" because she is Jewish. But there is yet a fourth story in this book. In the introduction to each of her subjects, the author introduces her own story of how the universal and the particular meet in her life, giving her book an important feminist twist. For all four, Jewish identity leads not to a narrow identity politics but to a more universal understanding of the common good.

With the past as prologue, the valuable lesson of the twentieth century is that identity politics represents a complex and fluid process that is engaged in a continual consciousness raising. It makes apparent both the obvious and the subtler processes that maintain hegemonic voices and practices. Harnessing the gains made through identity politics is not to abandon it, but rather to challenge, modify, and make explicit the hegemonic voices that claim to speak for us all. By so doing we achieve a common good not because we rid ourselves of our identity politics, but because such politics give voice to those who have been made invisible and unimportant, if not undesirable, in the cultural narrative that defines who "we" are.

> —Debra Renee Kaufman, Professor Emerita and Matthews
> Distinguished University Professor, Northeastern University
> July 3, 2020, Boston, Massachusetts

Notes

1. *New York Review of Books*, November 9, 2017, volume LXIV, number 17.
2. Chad Alan Goldberg, *Modernity and the Jews in Western Social Thought* (Chicago: University of Chicago Press, 2017).

PREFACE

T his book is about Jewish identity, but not religious observance. It is not about the ritualistic aspects of the Jewish religion, like keeping kosher or lighting candles on the eve before Sabbath. It is about Judaism as a religion of social justice. I am grateful to Ruth W. Messinger, who introduced me to the term *social justice Judaism* when I interviewed her in 2016 at the Utopia Diner in Manhattan. It was a concept Messinger learned from Rabbi Abraham Joshua Heschel, who taught at Jewish Theological Seminary where Messinger's mother worked as public relations director.[1]

Judaism's social justice message is what captured me as a teenager and young adult growing up in the midst of the Civil Rights Movement, the Anti-Vietnam War Movement, and the second wave Women's Movement. These movements jolted me into the awareness that many activists like myself came from Jewish backgrounds but did not openly identify themselves as Jewish.[2] The realization that we had an invisible Jewish identity in common thrust many of us into deeper bonding in study groups to explore the Jewish roots of the ethical value systems by which we had been raised and with which we were now engaging as feminist activists.[3]

Social justice Jews like myself may be found in all branches of Judaism—Reform, Conservative, Reconstructionist, Renewal, and Orthodox. What they have in common is that they all find primary spiritual meaning in relating to human beings regardless of nation, faith, ethnicity, sex, gender, or class. They are grounded in the belief that all life is sacred and that encounters with human beings should call forth our compassion and sense of justice.[4] There are also social justice Jews who hold these same universalist values but do not affiliate with any congregation. Some may be anti-organized religion or even self-defined agnostics and atheists.

Over the years, I have affiliated with Conservative, Reform, and Jewish Renewal congregations. Most recently I belonged to both a Reform congregation led by a social activist rabbi and to an eclectic Jewish fellowship called a *chavurah*, which is democratically led by its members instead of a rabbi, though a rabbi and cantor officiate during "High Holiday" Jewish New Year services. Both of these congregations practice sex, gender, and ethnic/racial equality.[5]

Like myself, the three Jewish women in my study—Gerda Lerner, Susana Wald, and Ruth W. Messinger—resonated with two fundamental social justice messages in the Jewish tradition. The first is that the stranger (*ger* in Hebrew), the one who is different, has much to contribute and should not be vilified. The second is that as Jews we are responsible for creating a better world where strangers are not treated as "others."[6] The contributions of these three universalist Jewish feminists need to be recognized for having changed the face of the fields in which they practiced.

Lerner is the Austrian-born scholar/activist who played a founding role in the creation of women's history. Wald is a Hungarian-born writer, translator, and internationally known feminist Surrealist artist. Messinger, initially a social worker and politician, was the first Jewish woman ever to run for mayor of New York City. She became president/chief executive officer of the American Jewish World Service in 1998, a global humanitarian organization. I selected these women for this study because their lives as Jews, like mine, illustrate two seemingly paradoxical strands in Judaism and human nature, namely universalism and particularism.

The universalism inherent in the Jewish tradition encourages peoples around the globe to sustain their own religio-ethnic-cultural group's customs and practices, without fear of being discriminated against or annihilated. A true universalism would therefore create the respect for difference that allows particularism to flourish. When particularism flourishes, different family networks and clans are able to practice their own culture, rituals, and customs according to their own belief systems. However, in order for particularism not to become extremism or tribal conflict between different clans and religio-ethnic-cultural groups, an overarching universalism needs also to operate simultaneously. During my 2016 interview with Ruth W. Messinger, she explained that she was raised to understand that Jewish particularity exists to teach universality.[7]

In these times of rising religious fundamentalisms that tend to separate human groups from one another, it seems more crucial than ever for faith traditions to emphasize their universal messages of compassion, empathy, and respect for difference to counter the fear of the "other" that has given rise to and normalized religious and nationalist extremism. This book will be of interest to Jews and non-Jews alike who believe the current climate can be improved by restoring the relationship among ethics, morality, and politics. It will also broaden the view of those who have not been sufficiently introduced to the social justice tradition within Judaism. Readers who wish to read further about these topics will find resources in the notes that go beyond the treatment of the three Jewish women in this study.

The shifts that have occurred in the public identities of these three Jewish women offer hope that when conditions in the world cry out for global human bonding, there will be leaders guided by universal values whose voices will not be muted. Will we hear them? Is the time now?

Notes

1. Interview with Ruth W. Messinger, October 21, 2016, Utopia Diner, Amsterdam Avenue and 73rd Street, New York, New York.
2. Stan Shaw Collection; https://archives.qc.cuny.edu/finding_aids/. See also Melody Li, "UConn Professor Emeritus Recalls March on Washington" (UConn, Neag School of Education, Nov. 7, 2013), https://education.uconn.edu/2013/11/07/uconn-professor-emeritus-recalls-march-on-washington/; Debra L. Schultz, *Going South: Jewish Women in the Civil Rights Movement* (New York: New York University Press, 2001); Melanie Kaye-Kantrowitz "To Be a Radical Jew in the Late 20th Century" in *The Tribe of Dina: A Jewish Women's Anthology*, , eds. Melanie Kaye-Kantrowitz and Irena Klepfisz (New York: Sinister Wisdom Books, 1986), 297–320. Joyce Antler, in *Jewish Radical Feminism: Voices From the Women's Liberation Movement* (New York: New York University Press, 2018), explores in the most thoroughgoing and

comprehensive way to date the phenomenon of Jewish feminists of the second wave being driven without conscious intention by values in their very varied Jewish backgrounds. See Antler's "Introduction" and "Part One: 'We Never Talked About It': Jewishness and Women's Liberation."

3. See examples of Jewish women bonding during the 1970s, 80s, and 90s as a result of second-wave feminism: Susan Weidman Schneider, founding editor-in-chief of *Lilith Magazine* since 1976 and author of *Jewish and Female: A Guide and Sourcebook for Today's Jewish Woman* (New York: Touchstone, 1985); Judith Plaskow, *Standing Again at Sinai: Judaism from a Feminist Perspective* (San Francisco: Harper, 1990); E.M. Broner, *The Telling: The Story of a Group of Jewish Women Who Journey to Spirituality Through Community and Ceremony* (San Francisco: Harper, 1993). Most recently, Antler interviewed scores of second-wave feminists after the fact of their second-wave activism, asking them to reflect on the influence of their Jewish backgrounds on their political lives. See Part Two of *Jewish Radical Feminism*, "'Feminism Enabled Me to Be a Jew': Identified Jewish Feminists."

4. The universalist outlook is expressed by many leading Jewish voices across the different branches of the religion. In Jewish Renewal, the universalist works of Rabbi Michael Lerner stand out, including *Jews and Blacks: A Dialogue on Race, Religion, and Culture in America* (New York: Plume, 1996), *The Left Hand of God: Taking Back Our Country From the Religious Right* (New York: Harper Collins, 2006), and *Revolutionary Love: A Political Manifesto to Heal and Transform the World* (Oakland, California: University of California Press, 2019). Jewish Renewal ordains women rabbis, like Tirzah Firestone, who at the time of her ordination was married to a non-Jew, a dramatic example of interfaith acceptance. See Firestone's memoir *With Roots in Heaven: One Woman's Passionate Journey into the Heart of Her Faith* (New York: Dutton, 1998). See also the following: Reform Rabbi Sidney Schwarz in *Judaism and Justice: The Jewish Passion to Repair the World* (Woodstock, Vermont: Jewish Lights 2006), Reform leaders Albert Vorspan and David Saperstein in *Jewish Dimensions of Social*

Justice: Tough Moral Choices of Our Time (New York: URJ Press, 1998), Modern Orthodox Rabbis Donniel Hartman in *Putting God Second: How to Save Religion from Itself* (Boston: Beacon Press, 2016), and Shmuly Yanklowitz in *The Soul of Jewish Social Justice* (Jerusalem: Urim Publications, 2014). Also see Conservative Rabbi Abraham Joshua Heschel in many works, including *The Prophets* (New York: Harper and Row, 1962) and *The Insecurity of Freedom* (New York: Schocken, 1972). In addition, the Reconstructionist Movement founded by Mordecai Kaplan views "Jewish people-hood" as "the particular vehicle for the expression and pursuit of universal values" according to Mel Scult in the introduction to the second paperback edition of Kaplan's *Judaism as a Civilization: Towards a Reconstruction of American-Jewish Life* (Philadelphia: Jewish Publication Society, 2010), viii.

5. I recently belonged to Temple Beth El, St. Petersburg, Florida, with Rabbi Michael Torop and Cantor Pamela Siskin; and to *Am HaYam* (People of the Sea), a Jewish Fellowship on Cape Cod, Massachusetts, where Rabbi Deanna Douglas and Cantor Elizabeth Anker officiate on High Holidays.

6. I remember these memorable lessons from reading the Torah (the Five Books of Moses) on my own as an adolescent, specifically Exodus 23:9, "You shall not oppress the stranger, for you know the feelings of a stranger, having yourselves been strangers in the land of Egypt." My adolescent impressions about the primacy of this message have been confirmed by rabbis, lay leaders, and scholars. Ruth W. Messinger cited that "the Torah reminds us at least thirty-five times to 'remember the stranger,' as we were strangers in a strange land" in Ruth W. Messinger, "Service Is My Way of Encountering God in the World, Since God Can Only Be Found in Our Response to the Needs of Others," *I Am Jewish: Personal Reflections Inspired by the Last Words of Daniel Pearl*, eds. Judea and Ruth Pearl (Woodstock, New York: Jewish Lights Publishing, 2004), 226. Reform Rabbi Deanna Douglas' Kol Nidre Service 2018 in Orleans, Massachusetts, cited seven biblical references to the *ger* and noted that "to be a Jew is to be a *ger*," meaning that Jews, the Hebrew people, were slaves in Egypt.

For a discussion of finding the roots of the term *Hebrew* in the second millennium BCE term *habiru* or *apiru*, roughly meaning "outsider," see Robert Wolfe "From Habiru to Hebrew: The Roots of the Jewish Tradition," *New English Review* (October 2009), http://www.newenglishreview.org/Robert_Wolfe/From_Habiru_to_Hebrews%3A_The_ Roots_of_the_Jewish_Tradition/.

7. Interview with Ruth W. Messinger, October 21, 2016.

INTRODUCTION

If I am not for myself, then who will be for me?
And if I am only for myself, then what am I?
And if not now, when?[1]

These words by Hillel, the great Talmudic rabbi and sage of the first century Before the Common Era (BCE), expressed a tension deeply seated in the human psyche. How can we arrive at the proper balance between self and community in order to lead an ethical life? If we reach beyond ourselves, whom do we consider part of our community? Is it those very much like us, or those who are also different?

In more recent times, sociologist Talcott Parsons formulated the dilemma in secular terms. He asked what variables motivate human beings to act socially, beyond the self. He answered that individuals move into the world toward others for two main reasons. First, they may wish to achieve a collective common good based on widely shared norms, following the imperative of universalism. Second, they may be motivated by personal relations with kinship, clan, and tribal networks, following the imperative of particularism.[2]

Both universalism and particularism are acknowledged in Jewish tradition and values and are illustrated in the lives and accomplishments of the three women presented in this work: Gerda Lerner, Susana Wald, and Ruth W. Messinger. Their respective fields are women's history, feminist Surrealist art, and international relations. Their lives and works as Jewish activists raise the question: Does Jewish identity call upon one to act with empathy toward others even at times when great numbers of fellow Jews feel the need to bond with one another solely as Jews?

Though I am younger by a generation or two than Lerner, Wald, and Messinger, nevertheless each of us was raised in the specter of World War II and the Holocaust, and the subsequent formation of Israel as a modern state. Like me, the women I am studying were faced with conflicts at different critical junctures in their lives that challenged them to decide to identify universally as Jewish citizens of the world, or particularly as Jews committed to Jewish communal unity. Should we devote ourselves to *tikkun olam*, the repair of the world, in the broadest global sense, or to the survival of Jewish belief and culture as embodied in Jewish institutions? Is a commitment to both possible?

Other important questions arise when considering the lives and works of the women in this study. Does a strict adherence to fostering bonds among all peoples of the world open one to criticism for betraying or erasing one's core Jewish identity, or for impeding Jewish continuity? Conversely, does an overexuberant fostering of one's own unique religion and/or ethnicity promote differences and distinctions among peoples, contributing to tribal and civil strife globally? Does such an attitude betray the overarching humanness of Jewish ethics?

According to Rabbi Sidney Schwarz in *Judaism and Justice*, the movements toward universalism and particularism were never completely divorced from one another in Jewish tradition, but rather coexisted on a continuum, the "Exodus-Sinai Continuum of Jewish Life." "Exodus consciousness" guides Jews and Jewish communities to act with group self-interest to maintain Jewish continuity, just as the ancient Hebrews, following God and Moses, freed themselves from slavery in Egypt. "Sinai consciousness," on the other hand, directs Jews to "aspire to altruistic, other-directed behavior in accordance with a pursuit of justice and a sense of sacred purpose," following mandates inherent in the Covenant received at Sinai.[3] Examples are the humane prohibitions against murder, adultery, theft, and false testimony.

Rabbi Schwarz rightly emphasizes the overlapping messages in both tendencies. The Exodus from Egypt, signifying particularism in the rescue of a singular people from oppression, contains at the same time "a cornerstone for Jewish universalism"[4]: "You shall not oppress a stranger . . . having yourselves been strangers in the land of Egypt" (Exodus 23:9). This proscription directs Jewish people to treat all others with equality and respect using the lesson of the Jewish experience of having been marginalized and dominated. It is this social justice message that first attracted me to Jewish identity, even though as an adolescent girl, I myself was being marginalized—I was not obligated as my brother was to study Hebrew or learn Jewish history.

Likewise, the universalist Covenant at Sinai also defines aspects of particularism in Jewish tradition, entailing "many customs that reinforce the distinctiveness of the Jewish people."[5] Examples include ethical monotheism, the Sabbath, and the prohibition of graven images.

Over the past century, several well-known individuals and organizations shifted the focus of their activism as Jews to different points along the Exodus-Sinai continuum. They did so in response to changing social, political, and economic conditions in the lives of Jewish people as a whole.

In general, when Jewish populations have been threatened by violence, pogroms, or ultimately genocide, as in the case of the Nazi Holocaust, Jewish leaders and organizations have for the most part been concerned with Exodus consciousness, the very survival of Jewish communities. Hannah Arendt, German refugee, philosopher, and Holocaust survivor, called times like these when Jewish populations were under attack periods when "the public sphere had ceased to function properly." At such times, Arendt saw the need for Jews to speak out publicly as Jews for Jewish continuity and survival, as she herself did in support of Zionism during the rise of the Third Reich.[6]

But after the establishment of Israel and the attainment of relative security of Jewish communities in the global diaspora, many Jewish leaders and organizations have often combined their particularist goals with greater Sinai consciousness, envisioning and bringing about unprecedented universalist projects by applying traditional Jewish values to the repair and improvement of world affairs.

Looking briefly at such shifts on the part of one Jewish humanitarian organization and two leading Jewish activists helps to provide a context for the ways that Lerner, Wald, and Messinger shifted their Jewish identities along the Exodus-Sinai continuum.

The shift from particular to universal concerns is reflected, for example, in the evolution of the Hebrew Immigrant Aid Society (HIAS). The Hebrew Immigrant Aid Society began in 1881 as a storefront on the lower East Side of Manhattan organized by American Jews to help other Jews fleeing anti-Semitic riots and pogroms in Russia and Eastern Europe. The expanding organization was responsible for rescuing hundreds of thousands of Jews following the two World Wars, offering safe haven, education, job training, and other resettlement services. But since the late 1970s, when the organization helped 3,600 Vietnamese, Cambodians, and Laotians to resettle in the United States following the fall of Saigon, HIAS has broadened its mission to help refugees no matter where their country of origin. Mark Hetfield, current president, has said, "HIAS doesn't help people because they are Jews, but because we are Jewish."[7]

Such shifts are reflected as well in the widening concerns addressed by American Zionist and social reformer Henrietta Szold. Szold was raised in late nineteenth-century Baltimore by traditional Jewish parents, her father a rabbi. She helped waves of Jewish refugees from Russian and Polish pogroms to settle in Baltimore, teaching them English and civics, an experience leading her eventually to become one of the most significant women Zionists to recognize that endangered Jews needed to have a permanent homeland. Often the only female on policy-making boards of Jewish scholars and educators, Szold founded Hadassah, the first Zionist organization of Jewish women, in 1912. Szold's example is particularly relevant to this study because she introduced the important element of gender into the Exodus-Sinai Continuum.[8]

Though Szold's commitment to Jewish continuity was always crystal clear—she spent the last twenty-five years of her life in Palestine working tirelessly on manifold projects—she nevertheless opposed the increasing militarism of Jewish leaders in Palestine against the Arabs, and she sided with Martin Buber and Rabbi Judah Magnes in favoring an Arab-Jewish binational state, even at the same time that she was directing Youth Aliah, the organization that saved thousands of Jewish children from Nazi Germany and Europe, bringing them to agricultural settlements in Palestine. Thus, Szold's concern for the "other"—for women and for Arabs—was an ingrained part of her universalism, her Sinai-Jewish consciousness.[9]

Impressive also is the broadening universalism of Holocaust survivor and spokesperson Elie Wiesel. A survivor of Auschwitz, Elie Wiesel played a critical role in associating the plight of Jews during the Holocaust with the later struggles of oppressed Jews in other parts of the world, such as Russia, Arab lands, and Ethiopia. Eventually though, his Holocaust experience underscored for him the Jewish value "not to stand idly by" when any group, anywhere, was being persecuted. In the 1980s, he called upon the national Jewish community in the United States to oppose apartheid in South Africa, and even earlier, in 1978, when he was appointed by President Carter to serve as chair of the President's Commission on the Holocaust, he strongly endorsed the recommendation of a Committee of Conscience to serve as a first alert against future genocides anywhere in the world.[10]

Like Elie Weisel and Henrietta Szold, Gerda Lerner, Susana Wald, and Ruth W. Messinger were raised in Jewish households where the lessons of the Exodus from Egypt and the Covenant received at Sinai were significant parts of the tradition they inherited. Like Weisel and Szold, they often resolved their conflicts and divided loyalties about social action by moving beyond "either/or" options to find original ways of contributing to their fields.

Lerner and Wald both experienced and survived the Nazi occupation of their countries, Austria and Hungary respectively, as secular and assimilated urban Jews. They each emigrated to the Americas with a heightened sense of their vulnerability as Jews under fascism and felt the need to determine when and where their Jewishness could safely be revealed. Nevertheless, they found different ways to serve the common good by subtly channeling certain key Jewish values at the core of their identities.

For Lerner, as we shall see, the ethical values of Judaism found their way into her anti-fascist writing, political organizing, research, scholarship, and teaching. For Wald, symbols of spiritual connection that had to be hidden under occupation—for example, candle lighting and Torah chanting—became primary sources of optimism and faith leading her to visual art, ritual, and myth as means of changing public consciousness. In these ways, the responses of Lerner and Wald as Holocaust survivors differ from that of Elie Wiesel, an observant Jew, who asserted a public Jewish identity throughout his writings, teachings, and community service.

Messinger, the youngest of the three profiled here, was born in Manhattan, raised by Polish/German Jewish parents, and educated in universalist approaches to Conservative Judaism under the influence of Rabbi Abraham Joshua Heschel. Her beginnings resemble those of Henrietta Szold in that rabbinic teachings were woven into both of their upbringings in urban city centers of the United States. Both of them also left more secular pursuits to become public Jewish leaders in later life with humanitarian messages to communicate about the place of Jews in the larger world. Messinger's profile examines her deep identification with Jewish values that she was able to express publicly by taking the leadership of the American Jewish World Service (AJWS). In keeping with her upbringing that Jewish particularity teaches universality, she said the following after having made her first trip to El Salvador as president/chief executive officer of AJWS:

> This model of Judaism—the idea that Jews are responsible for building a better world—was the type of Judaism I was raised with. This was a chance for me to be in Jewish circles and say, "Here's something new, different and important that Jews are doing and should be doing more of in the world."[11]

Indirectly, all three women—Lerner, Wald, and Messinger—were following Hillel's second question: "And if I am only for myself, then what am I?" Ultimately, all three women have acted as universalist feminists applying Jewish values to the repair of the world. In so doing, they have changed the way we understand the fields of history, art, and international relations.

Notes

1. Ethics of the Fathers (*Pirkei Avot*) 1.4; see www.chabad.org/library/article_cdo/aid/682498/jewish/English-Text.htm.
2. Talcott Parsons, *The Social System* (London: Routledge and Kegan Paul, 1951). See also Ruth A. Wallace and Alison Wolff, *Contemporary Sociological Theory: Continuing the Classical Tradition*, 4th ed. (Englewood Cliffs, New Jersey: Prentice Hall, 1995), 34.
3. Schwarz, *Judaism and Justice.* See xxvi, 25–26, and especially Chapter 16, "Reconciling Exodus and Sinai," 239 *ff.*

4. Ibid., 25–26.

5. Ibid.

6. Deborah Barer, "Between Public and Private: Navigating the Jewishness of Hannah Arendt," academia.edu/1689003/. Based on Hannah Arendt, *The Human Condition* (Chicago: University of Chicago Press, 1958).

7. See https://www.hias.org/history and https://www.hias.org/leadership/mark-hetfield.

8. Marvin Lowenthal, *Henrietta Szold: Life and Letters* (New York: The Viking Press, 1942), 36–54. Also see Michael Brown, "Henrietta Szold 1860–1945"; https://jwa.org/encylcopedia/article/szold-henrietta.

9. Eyal Chowers "The Late Blooming Vision of Henrietta Szold," *Dissent,* March 29, 2012; dissentmagazine.org/onlinearticles/the_late_blooming_vision_of_henrietta_szold.

10. Schwarz, *Judaism and Justice,* 134–5.

11. Ruth W. Messinger qtd. in *Messinger of Hope: A Portrait of Ruth W. Messinger* by Angela Cave (New York: American Jewish World Service, 2016), 24.

1

GERDA LERNER (APRIL 30, 1920–JANUARY 2, 2013)

Personal Association

I became aware of Gerda Lerner's scholarship in 1977–78, when for the second time I taught mainly Black, Latino, and Latina students. I used Lerner's groundbreaking documentary anthology *Black Women in White America* (1972)[1] as the dominant text in my writing classes in the Franconia External Degree Program (FRED). Lerner's collection was one of the first books to detail the contributions of Black women to American history. It paved the way for the development of the field of Black Women's History.

My students were paraprofessionals in human service fields who needed to obtain bachelor's degrees in order to keep their jobs. I taught them thesis writing and institutional analysis by traveling across New England to their workplaces—schools, hospitals, and social service agencies—to supervise their research. Most of my students were women—teachers' aids, nurses' assistants, and lab workers. They appreciated the materials Lerner had gathered, many previously unpublished, documenting Black women's heroic efforts to organize self-help networks and to sustain their human dignity.

It was only later, when I became a teacher of Women's Studies (1978–86) at the University of Buffalo, that I learned more of Lerner's refugee past: her being deported from Nazi-occupied Austria in 1939 and becoming, in the United States in the late 1960s, one of the pioneering founders of Women's History across lines of class, ethnicity, race, and culture.

Lerner is most well-known for focusing on the important ways women throughout history continually resisted victimization under race- and class-biased, male-dominated systems. During the 1970s, many radical feminists were stressing the oppression and subjugation of women by patriarchy.[2] Instead, Lerner's scholarship emphasizes women's agency, their coming to feminist consciousness, and the ways women of different cultures, ethnicities, races, and classes empowered themselves through organizing for women's rights and racial and economic equality, especially in the United States.[3]

As one of the founders of the field of Women's History, Lerner ensured its continuity through promoting the establishment of Women's History Month in the United States. She launched the first master's and doctoral programs in the field of Women's History at Sarah Lawrence College and the University of Wisconsin-Madison, respectively.[4]

In Women's Studies at the University of Buffalo, as in the FRED program, I worked with colleagues who, like Gerda Lerner, were secular Jews with universalist perspectives. They saw the fight against anti-Black racism as linked with the fight against anti-Semitism. Prior to that, though, I worked with more mainstream, traditional Jewish colleagues who tended to focus exclusively on combating anti-Semitism to the exclusion of other causes. They often experienced me as splitting the ranks because of my commitment as a Jew to ending anti-Black racism. As I was writing this book, I learned that Lerner had also been vulnerable to similar criticisms.[5]

My being accused of splitting the Jewish ranks as a teacher occurred the first time I taught English to mainly Black, Latino, and Latina students in 1967–69 at Lefferts Junior High School in Crown Heights, Brooklyn. This was the same time the New York City's United Federation of Teachers (UFT) went on strike over community control of schools. The Community School Board in the mainly Black neighborhood next to mine in Brooklyn, Ocean Hill-Brownsville, peremptorily fired teachers the board did not think were equipped to teach their youngsters.[6] The dismissed teachers were almost all Jewish, as were most of the teachers in my school who joined the strike. Many African-Americans accused the UFT of being "Jewish-dominated,"[7] UFT President Albert Shanker being Jewish and the UFT chapter chairman in Ocean Hill-Brownsville being Jewish as well.[8]

I was expected to join the strike because I was new to my school and a recent college graduate who had never taught before. And I was Jewish. However, in the few months before the strike, I came to separate myself from the school's majority of Jewish teachers because they seemed to be more concerned with issues of discipline than with empowering students to learn. They were not inclined, as I was, to encourage the students to develop within themselves the Black pride that the Black faculty in the school were encouraging.

My strike breaking caused me to lose my job about a year later, though teaching small classes during the strike was the most meaningful time I ever spent with my students. Their parents encouraged them to attend the classes being taught by fewer than ten teachers—all the Black faculty and two other Jewish teachers besides myself. All of us engaged the students in reading contemporary Black authors and discussed current events with them. Had Lerner's *Black Women in America* been available then, I probably would have used it with my seventh through ninth graders.

Like mine, Lerner's identification with marginalized "others" different from herself was an extension and affirmation of her Jewishness. She had learned to connect her own vulnerability as a Jew under fascism and Nazi anti-Semitism to others who were also targets of discrimination. In the United States, that meant workers, women, and Blacks.

Lerner's positive identification with American Blacks began her first year in Manhattan when she walked across town to Sydenham Hospital in Harlem where she worked and trained to be an X-ray technician. Sydenham was a Black hospital where, Lerner explains in her political autobiography *Fireweed*, she "dealt with the injured, the sick, the disturbed." She took her lunches in the parks "with black mothers and their children or with homeless idlers on park benches," and she "never felt alienation or hostility or danger." As a new refugee in New York, she perceived Blacks as much more outgoing and friendly than other people.[9] She appreciated their "liveliness," much as she had appreciated the boisterous sounds of working-class people in the Karl Marx Hof houses she had passed on her walks to school as a youngster in Vienna.[10]

Lerner became critical of assimilated Jews in the United States, whose blending in to dominant, white Protestant society included their gaining privileges from institutionalized racial segregation that discriminated against American Blacks in the workforce and the housing market.[11] Like I did, she probably asked herself the question, "Why aren't more Jews in the United States connecting the racism against Blacks with the ways Jews throughout history have been scapegoated?" For me, racial segregation had created a systemic problem in education—segregated schools without sufficient numbers of faculty of color for students to look up to as role models and curricula that did not sufficiently encourage Black self-empowerment.

In studying more of Lerner's life, I wished to understand how she navigated being able to use her privilege as an academic professional not only to do what was good for the Jews, but also to encourage the success of others, such as Blacks and working-class women, without abandoning her Jewish identity.

In her essay "A Weave of Connections," published in 1997, Lerner wrote, "I am a historian because of my Jewish experience."[12] It was the verbatim response she had given in the early 1990s to Joyce Antler, a social and cultural historian, when Antler invited her to speak at a conference on the subject of U.S. Jewish women's history at Brandeis. However, this considered response by Lerner only followed upon her initial retort, "I never thought about it." Indeed, as a pioneering historian of women for a quarter century, Lerner had not written directly of Jewish women's experience. Antler's challenge prompted Lerner to self-examine and set in motion not only the talk that Lerner presented at the conference, but also her book *Why History Matters*, which includes "A Weave of Connections" and several other essays which examine the influence of Jewishness on her work as a historian.

The essays explain that Lerner's simultaneous outsider status under Nazi fascism as a Jew, a woman, and an exile inclined her attention toward other outsiders in the United States whose experiences had not yet been written into history. Lerner considered American Blacks to be America's most targeted outsiders, not Jews.

Nevertheless, the question remained: How could Lerner be a historian because of her Jewish experience but not write about Jewish women's history? In "A Weave of Connections," Lerner implied that for her to have written about Jewish women would have been too particularist, marking her as concerned only with her own religious and ethnic identity and with Israeli nationalism. It made sense for her, she argued, to transcend identity politics and write about other marginalized women.[13] But, of course, the women she chose to write about need not have been either/or. I believe the emotional reasons behind her avoidance of Jewish women's history were secret even to her at that time, and the organized Jewry practiced in her Vienna childhood did not meet the universal goals and values of the Jewish tradition which she admired in her pre-adulthood and internalized as ideals for herself.

How then *did* she weave Jewish universalism into the entire body of her life's work as a feminist activist even without writing about Jewish women? How did anti-Semitic conditions sometimes converge in the United States—during the Cold War and the outbreak of the first *intifada* in Israel—to cause Lerner to relive the depth and volatility of anti-Jewish bias that had flared up in Europe? How did rises in anti-Semitism cause her to rethink the effectiveness of universalism as a strategy for creating a world safe for all minorities?

Resisting Jewish Victimization: Becoming Political, Not Religious

Lerner's championing of resistance on the part of women, minorities, and the working classes was rooted in her experience as a Jewish adolescent in 1930s Vienna when fascists and then Nazis came to power and persecuted Jews as inferior outsiders, deviant "others." The fascist attempts to humiliate and victimize Jews forced Lerner "to take a position, to assert or deny" who she was.[14] Lerner's response was to identify with the Viennese Jewish community in the many heroic ways she watched it organize daily to resist while it was under attack:

> Ever since that time I have known about the strength of the powerless to check those in power. I have never believed those versions of history and those representations of reality that present the world from the point of view of the powerful. My childhood taught me the wisdom and effectiveness of resistance and the

necessity of skepticism toward the values of those who made the rules.[15]

Lerner was being trained in an Orthodox synagogue for a *bat mitzvah* in 1934, a year after the right-wing clerical party under Chancellor Engelbert Dollfuss took power from the Social Democrats and began cracking down on religious freedom.[16] The Jewish instruction she received from a rabbi in public elementary school under the Social Democrats had ended, and she now sat in classrooms where crucifixes hung. Her congregation responded by affirming their unity with one another: "We had to stick together because THEY hated us. We had to stick together because we were surrounded by enemies. We had to show that we were proud of our faith. We had to be good to show that Jews could be good."[17]

Lerner later wrote about the deep-seated character of Jewish bonding in times of stress in her sweeping tome *The Creation of Patriarchy*.[18] There she describes how—as early as chapters 15 and 17 of the Book of Genesis—the uniting of the Hebrew tribes under Abram's leadership would endow them not only with divine blessing, but also with future well-being if they remained loyal to monotheism in the face of the widespread, goddess-centered polytheism surrounding them in the ancient world. The Hebrew God promises Abram and his generations future prosperity, land, and offspring if they continue to worship their one invisible God and to mark their bond through circumcision. God adds to the significance of the ritual by changing Abram's name to Abraham. "Thus every Jew is born into a historical world," Lerner wrote in "A Weave of Connections," referring to God's promise to Abraham of a better future for his generations. And every Jew is also born with "a consciousness of being linked to other members of the Jewish community."[19]

Ultimately, however, organized Judaism presented a problem for Lerner in its legacy of patriarchy, which is marked by the divine blessing being bestowed only upon males. In "A Weave of Connections," Lerner pointed out that had she been a boy in Vienna in the 1920s and 30s, she would have been studying Talmud, Mishna, and Midrash: "I would have learned Jewish history in a positive way. I would have learned about the existence of wise rabbis and great leaders," but "I was a girl," and this aspect of Jewish learning "was out of my reach."[20]

Lerner's Jewish congregation treated boys and girls differently. Though her parents, Ilona and Robert Kronstein, were both assimilated, mostly nonobservant Jews, the family belonged to an Orthodox congregation due to the influence of Lerner's paternal grandmother, Grandmama, in whose spacious house Lerner, her parents, and her younger sister lived, in the apartment above Grandmama's.[21]

The Jewish congregation to which the Kronstein family belonged separated boys and girls during religious services, preventing them from participating equally. Boys and girls were also treated differently when the ages for their *bar* and *bat mitvahs* were being determined—thirteen for boys, but fourteen for girls.[22]

The youngster Gerda Kronstein was sensitive to gender equality because her mother had a great deal of independence in her marriage. Ilona was an unconventional artist/intellectual who kept separate quarters in their apartment for privately entertaining her friends and acquaintances. Ilona had become deeply ambivalent about marriage and motherhood once she and Robert began living in Robert's mother's house, and after giving birth to Gerda, she had a difficult time nursing. Ilona convinced Robert to draw up a legal agreement to define their separate lives.[23]

Ilona's need for a private life, and her consequent conflicts with her husband and mother-in-law, strained her relationship with Gerda, who felt deprived of mothering. Gerda's younger sister, Nora, whom Ilona named after Ibsen's proto-feminist heroine in *A Doll's House*, received more pampering than Gerda. In Gerda Lerner's autobiography, she wrote—identifying herself in the third person—that her mother's "unavailability was the predominant theme of those years, and so the child, frequently disappointed and rebuffed, finally transferred allegiance to the governess."[24]

At age ten, after Ilona fired a nanny to whom Gerda was very attached, probably due to Ilona's feelings of inadequacy as a mother and loss of control, Gerda decided "to depend emotionally on no one," she wrote in her autobiography. "I would try to make it without a father, without a mother. Just on my own."[25]

Gerda's wished-for closeness to her mother became realized during the political battle for control of Austria in 1933 between the Social Democrats, whom Ilona supported, and Dollfuss' clerical party. At the dinner table, during political conversations about the clerical party's victory, Ilona described the clerical party as "reactionary and secretly anti-Semitic," saying it "did not believe in the rights of working people and tried to foist their religious ideas on everyone."[26] By age thirteen, Gerda had personally experienced these religious changes at school.

The dinner discussions resulted in a greater rift between Ilona and Robert. Gerda identified more strongly with her mother's concern for the well-being of the powerless and poor.[27] Robert was a successful pharmacist whose leanings were more bourgeois. As an employer, he was irked that Ilona was defending trade unions and told her "she didn't know what she was talking about" since "she hadn't worked a day in her life."[28]

One can speculate that even as Gerda yearned for more of her mother's attention and affection, these conversations highlighted her mother's limited power as a wife and mother in 1930s Vienna. Not having harmony between her parents, Lerner championed her mother's side which was more consistent with her own sympathies for the poor and working classes. Thus, Gerda's attachment to a liberal political agenda reflected in large measure the need she had to be recognized and acknowledged by her unconventional mother, whom she viewed as an intellectual committed to democracy and equality.

"At age fourteen," Gerda Lerner wrote, "the personal became political for me," and "in the years between fourteen and seventeen, my relationship with my mother grew in depth and intensity." Ilona invited her daughter to join the teatime discussions she hosted in her studio among "a circle of young and poor artists and writers" who treated the young Lerner's contributions to their talk as intelligent: "I . . . learned that I could, if I tried, be considered clever by intellectuals, and so I read avidly, thought deeply and tried to produce cynical bon mots . . . My life-long love of art comes from this adolescent experience, as does my writing."[29]

By showing Lerner an alternate model to that of the middle-class housewife and mother, Ilona's example freed Lerner to pay attention to the political sphere. The proto-fascist Engelbert Dollfuss was rescinding many rights and freedoms as Chancellor, not only religious freedom. He was abandoning the parliamentary democracy that had existed in Austria under the Social Democrats. Lerner saw freedom of the press and the right to jury trials become annulled. She saw the right of assembly suspended. Likewise, workers' rights and trade unions were curtailed.[30]

To oppose Dollfuss, Ilona moved further toward Communism, causing Robert to experience his wife's allegiances as increasing the family's vulnerability, especially as Jews. However, Ilona's Communist leanings only drew Lerner closer to her mother and made her more sensitive to workers and the poor.[31]

On Lerner's walks to school, she passed the residences of the less fortunate—the well-known Karl Marx Hof houses created by the Social Democrats, the Socialist Workers' Home, and the orphanage where some Jewish children lived. She was attracted to the "giggles" of the children's play, "as if the poor did not know they were poor."[32] However, her father had "programmed" her "to socialize only with children who came from suitable families" since he looked down upon "lower-class occupations" and wouldn't allow her to invite the Jewish children from the orphanage to their home.[33]

Lerner was ill at ease with her father's biases that conflicted with the Jewish value of charity toward the poor, a value she learned not only at home, but also in her congregation and from instruction at school under the Social Democrats. She became further disturbed when members of her congregation would not seat the poor during High Holiday services, or when her grandmother resisted buying eggs from the poor woman who sold eggs to the congregation. Lerner asked herself how Jews could see themselves as being charitable toward the poor and working classes if they excluded them unfairly.[34]

Lerner focused her growing doubts about organized religion "on the hypocrisy and injustice" she observed in her own congregation—the lack of charity to needy poor people in their midst and the division between the genders that she perceived as unfair. In the end, Lerner decided she could not go through with the *bat mitzvah* for which she had been studying. Becoming a *bat mitzvah* signified the Jewish girl's being accepted as an adult member of the Jewish community. But this Jewish community had disappointed her. "The decision not to be bat mitzvahed was truly my coming of age. . . . By the time I was fourteen, I had become a political person." Lerner's decision was also a defining moment in her relation to organized Judaism: "The community I had tried to find among . . . my co-religionists had disillusioned me."[35]

Instead, Lerner found community among other politicized young people, often those at school, Communists advocating for the poor and working classes who were also fighting against Dollfuss' fascist acts, such as placing the leaders of former left-wing parties and trade unions in internment camps and jails.[36]

By rejecting her congregation, Lerner may have also been responding out of fear. The political situation for Jews was becoming more dire because the Austrian Nazis, who had been forced underground, rose up to seize power in the *putsch* of July 1934 and assassinated Dollfuss. Though they failed, Dollfuss' successor, Kurt von Schuschnigg, was a more reactionary clerical fascist who then made Catholicism the official religion of state.[37]

When the Nazis were finally successful in bloodlessly taking over Austria in 1938, the Catholic country's anti-Semitism was more virulently unleashed. Jews were now humiliated on the streets daily; they were fired from positions in business, government, and university; their businesses were raided and stolen from, and they were imprisoned on trumped-up charges such as "unpatriotic activity."[38] Many people in Lerner's circle knew of Jews who committed suicide to avoid imprisonment.[39]

In this more violent, anti-Semitic atmosphere, it became difficult for Jews to gather together for mutual assistance and support. Simply grouping together in synagogues for communal activities was often dangerous. Armed Nazi gangs would force men from synagogues to use their prayer shawls to wash the floors and toilet bowls of local SS headquarters. They would force the elderly on the streets who looked Jewish to do knee bends until they collapsed.[40]

Members of the Jewish community now had to resort to other, seemingly self-abnegating means to avoid torture— "to make oneself inconspicuous, to blend into a crowd, to make no eye contact with anyone, to call no attention to oneself." Prevented by oppressive conditions from garnering support from one another as members of the Jewish community, Jews practiced self-preservation and invisibility as individuals.

When Lerner reflected years later on these behaviors, she did not view these individuals as victims. Rather, she saw them as brave, having the "daily courage" to venture into public areas, pretending "one was still a person with some rights as a citizen or human being."[41]

Without her parents' knowledge, Lerner joined a diverse community of Communist student groups that were committed to the independence from Germany of a democratic Austria. She feared that her activities, if discovered, could endanger her family. However, it was her father who was targeted by the Nazis for being a Jewish entrepreneur. Moreover, when one of his female workers had been jailed for being a Communist, he made himself more vulnerable by continuing to pay her salary.[42] Within weeks after the Nazis annexed Austria, armed men in SA uniforms entered Lerner's home. The Nazis demanded of Lerner, her mother, her grandmother, and her younger sister to know the whereabouts of Lerner's father, who had narrowly escaped a few days before to neutral Liechtenstein, the small principality on the Rhine between Germany, Austria, and Switzerland.[43]

When Hitler came to power in Germany in 1933, Lerner's father had the foresight to establish a satellite pharmacy in Liechtenstein in the event his family would be endangered and forced to emigrate from Austria. Less than a month after the first raid on the Kronstein home, a second raid occurred. This time, Viennese police came into the household, interrogated all the women, and imprisoned Gerda and her mother. The police held them hostage, thinking they could blackmail Lerner's father into signing away his property and his business.[44] But Lerner's father remained in Liechtenstein unapprehended for the duration of the war.

In prison, Lerner and her mother were separated, but Ilona, who exhibited bravery during the ordeal, found clandestine ways to communicate with her daughter.[45] For Lerner, the "hours, days, weeks" of her several-month incarceration became "the most important events" of her life. They gave it "a meaning and shape" she "ever since tried to comprehend."[46]

The lesson she learned in prison was the one she would emphasize throughout her feminist scholarship. In order to survive in the Austrian civil prison cell that was built for one but that she shared at times with four others, she could not allow herself to be a "victim": "Victims didn't survive. They could go mad or be beaten to death or starve and choose their own form of death, but if you wanted to survive you could not do it alone and you had to fight with all your strength to keep some sort of social contract." In her cell, she was able to participate in a "fragile community of survival" composed of women who were imprisoned because, like her, they were Jews, or they were considered "other" by the Nazis because they were working-class Socialists.[47]

Lerner formulated in prison the idea that the survival of the marginalized depended upon bonding with others across lines of religion, race, and class. This same theme gained her repute as an historian after she graduated from Columbia in 1966 and published her major works on women under patriarchy.

Refugee, Not Immigrant

Lerner and her mother could be released from prison only on the condition that they be deported. Ilona, who had directed all her energy in prison to maintaining her hopes, left prison exhausted and unable to function.[48]

The extensive, complicated bureaucratic processes involved in securing appropriate papers for leaving Austria, devised by Adolf Eichmann, were meant to degrade and wear down the Viennese Jews, whose days and hours spent on endless lines presaged the lines of forced marches from the cattle cars.[49] Lerner wrote years later about having been deported from her native country:

> To be helpless and without a foundation of rights and recognized status is . . . shattering. . . . It is not only a matter of being suddenly de-classed; it is a matter of suddenly being a nonperson. A person without rights and citizenship is a person without self-definition. . . . The refugee lives from day to day, from hour to hour and throws out lines across the fog: pipedreams, fantasies, bragging tales, long-range plans. All for nothing, for the only skill worth learning is adaptability. Learn to travel light is the basic refugee wisdom.[50]

In September 1938, two months before Kristallnacht (November 9–10),[51] when in Austria, Germany, and parts of Czechoslovakia,

members of the Nazi party would be joined by civilians to torch synagogues and vandalize Jewish shops as police and firefighters looked on,
Lerner, her mother, and her younger sister left Austria to meet Lerner's
father in Vaduz, Liechtenstein. There the immediate family reunited
for a short period. The reunion could not be permanent, however, since
Lerner's father's residence as a pharmacist was temporary and required
monthly renewal. To safeguard their status, the family could not openly
discuss their refugee status or their being Jewish. Ilona "had to fit in"
as the pharmacist's wife, a role that she felt she had escaped in Social
Democratic Austria.[52]

Lerner witnessed her family become fragmented once more. Her
sister was sent to a Swiss boarding school; her mother, ill-equipped and
unwilling to keep up bourgeois appearances, migrated to France, while
her father remained in Liechtenstein. Lerner herself hoped to marry a
Viennese fellow Communist who was working as a doctor in New York
City and whose family helped her procure the proper emigration documents. She wouldn't see her father again until after World War II. But
immediately before Lerner embarked for the United States, she visited
her mother briefly in Cagnes, expecting that somehow, in some way, she
could convince her mother to obtain a visa to come to the United States.[53]

Their meeting was fraught with intense emotional conflict, since
unbeknownst to Lerner, Ilona was living with a younger man, a writer
whom Lerner believed was using her mother for his own ends. Lerner
asked herself, "What if something like this were to happen in America?"[54]
Lerner wanted to save her mother from the debilitating situation, but
when she confronted her mother, Ilona defended her romantic partner
and refused to be judged by her daughter, whom she accused of being
jealous.[55]

Still intent on saving her mother, given the dangers of Ilona's stateless-
ness and her being a foreigner in France during a time of encroaching war,
Lerner vowed, upon leaving Cagnes, to bring her mother to the United
States once she got settled. Lerner's autobiography records the new levels
of feelings their relationship then entailed:

> Our visit had been so difficult, so full of good intentions badly
> carried out, so charged with misunderstandings and tensions, that
> I felt unable to free myself from its complexities. . . . I wanted, I

needed desperately to straighten matters out between us, to make our relationship as close, as passionately intimate as it had been. Yet I seemed to see her in a new light, with an ever more critical eye. I was out of step with her needs, her despair, her efforts at finding the right direction. And she had no concept of my life in America, so that our letters, with all their old intense words of intimacy, were tragically out of touch.[56]

Lerner's correspondence with her mother lasted from 1939, the year Lerner left Europe, to 1941 when Ilona, ill with multiple sclerosis, finally returned to Lichtenstein at her husband's urging.[57] In her letters, Ilona was at times desperate to join her daughter in the United States, as when she escaped from the Gurs detention camp in 1940, where she and other women without French citizenship had been held without adequate provisions for survival. Ilona lived hand-to-mouth in Gurs without any assurance that she could keep up with or meet the ever-changing quotas and requirements for emigration to the United States.[58] In August 1940, Ilona wrote to her daughter, "Send food. Send money. Do something . . . I have nothing, no hope," and shortly thereafter, "Get new affidavits. Send letters of support to the Consul. Contact relief agencies."[59]

Reading these pleas made Lerner feel that she was "killing" her mother, she writes in her autobiography. Yet, she also realized she was hardly in a position to help herself at the time.[60] Lerner felt that both her mother and father had no idea what her actual situation was in the United States—no wealthy contacts to serve as sponsors, no influence with the State Department, no access to relief agencies or refugee support networks. Even so, Lerner tried to secure affidavits and letters of support for her parents. She even wrote to Mrs. Roosevelt to intercede on behalf of her mother. She was turned down everywhere and came to realize that in the United States, immigration was actually being discouraged.[61]

Lerner's inability to fulfill her promise to bring her mother to America and her great ambivalence about feeling responsible for her saddened and haunted her for her entire life. Only in analysis decades later did she acknowledge the emotional costs of having repressed her guilt about feeling that she had abandoned her mother.[62] Her failure to help her mother may have combined with other ghosts in her past to block her from writing about her life as a Jew in Europe in her scholarship. Their time together in Cagnes was the last time Lerner and her mother saw each other. The epithet "survivor guilt" has become an overused abstraction. But in reality, learning the complex, concrete circumstances of Lerner's arrangements to save her mother that went awry enables us to grasp the wrenching anguish and regret she carried forward when she remembered all her failed attempts.

Lerner may not have anticipated that the powerless refugee without rights whom she had become after her Viennese imprisonment would indelibly remain with her as an internalized shadow self, even after she settled with her fiancé in New York. Only women already married to United States' citizens could enter the country according to the Mann Act of 1910, so she was threatened with deportation a second time when she reached Ellis Island engaged but not yet married. This time she could have been deported back to Austria, where she would surely be sent to a concentration camp. Her fiancé's relatives narrowly saved her from this fate by vouching for her pledge to produce marriage papers within the week, despite Lerner's uncertainty about marrying a man to whom she had become engaged mainly for political reasons. She did produce the papers and marry Bobby Jensen, but after a year and a half, the marriage ended. Lerner realized that her goal to become an American citizen was at odds with her husband's desire to join his political comrades, mainly German-speaking, anti-fascist refugees, when they returned to their homelands after fascism was destroyed.[63]

Lerner spent two years in New York as a refugee struggling to survive (1939–41). She felt compelled to maintain a low profile as a Jew, not even seeking the assistance of agencies like the Hebrew Immigrant Aid Society for fear it could be dangerous to her status.[64] Was she perhaps recalling those Jews on the streets of Vienna under the Nazis who did not dare to congregate with other Jews in community for fear of becoming more visible targets of oppression?

Lerner moved to California with her second husband, Carl Lerner, a Jew and a Communist screenwriter, whom she met in New York through her work as a refugee youth group education director. Her relationship with Carl was a loving, lifelong relationship. Carl criticized what he called Gerda's "underground mentality." It was inappropriate, he thought, for her to live in hiding, as it were, in the United States because "everyone had the right to their convictions; everyone had the right of free speech and free association." But these ideas sounded naive to Lerner, whose scarring refugee experiences put her in a constant state of fear. She thought she knew better. She knew the rights of the "other" could dissolve in an instant if fascism should take over. She wanted to do nothing to jeopardize her chance of becoming an American citizen. For her, "being refugee-smart meant understanding exactly the difference between" herself "and native-born Americans." Initially, in California, she would join no progressive political organizations, not attend their meetings, not sign their petitions.[65]

Because Lerner's was a German passport, her official status became "enemy alien" a month after the United States entered World War II. She was required to register, be fingerprinted, and report monthly to her local federal post office. She resented the government's making no distinction between German and Austrian. Further, no distinction was made between immigrants who were German citizens and Jewish refugees who, like Lerner, were *fleeing* Nazism. This racist policy placed immigrants in the enemy category simply based on their German nationality or on ethnicity similar to German, instead of on political conviction.[66] Once again, a government was labeling Lerner as "enemy" and requiring her to be documented, only this time the government was not Germany but the United States.

Lerner's critique of the United States deepened when she witnessed the racist treatment of the Japanese during the war. All West Coast Japanese nationals, including children, and all persons of Japanese origin were relocated and sent to camps, their being processed in long lines in front of barracks recalling for her with terror the deportations of Jews from Austria.[67]

American Radical and Communist

Lerner became a naturalized citizen in 1943. She thought of the United States as "the best model for democratic governance yet devised by human beings," but believed it was in need of "improvement."[68] Early on, her fears about discrimination in the United States were reinforced when she held her first regular job on Fifth Avenue as a salesgirl in a fancy candy store. To be hired and earn the twelve dollars per week that was the minimum wage in 1940, Lerner had to hide her Jewishness, even though the owners were, like her, Jewish emigrés from Vienna. As well-to-do *assimilated* Jews, they wanted only Protestant women selling to their élite clientele. On the other hand, the workers in the candy *factory* were all Jewish refugees who worked illegally for below minimum wage, a detail Lerner learned from an intimidated factory worker who made daily deliveries. After Lerner reported the violation to the Labor Department, she was immediately fired, her bosses figuring that she had been the informant.[69]

If being an assimilated Jew in the United States meant discriminating against the poor, even when the poor shared your background as a persecuted, religious minority, Lerner was not interested in joining the ranks of assimilated Jews.

Lerner was already familiar with the behaviors of Jews who did not want their religious differences to be offensive to the dominant culture in which they lived. The members of the Kronstein family in Austria, the family on her father's side, were the kind of Jews who assimilated in public, attempting to blend in with Viennese Catholic culture. Lerner's immediate family did not keep kosher. They spoke High German, not Yiddish, the Jewish folk language. Lerner's father encouraged her and her sister not to "act Jewish," meaning not to fit certain stereotypes, like speaking with their hands, raising their voices, or being too inquisitive. For Lerner, these behaviors involved a kind of self-erasure or denial that she experienced as "a corrosive poison."[70] It must have been difficult for Lerner to safeguard her status in the United States as a Jew by keeping a low Jewish profile, especially since she was committed to resisting self-denial and her own sense of victimization. She must have experienced much inner anguish and turmoil.

After Lerner and her husband, Carl, moved to California, Carl eventually found work in and around Los Angeles as a film editor. Carl was already a Communist when Lerner met him, and she, as an anti-fascist who had lived more than half her life under dictatorships, wanted "to be introduced to the true progressive America."[71] She saw no contradiction in "a firm allegiance" to the United States "and its Constitution" and the Communist desire to improve "the social system."[72]

Though Carl identified strongly with the unionization of film workers, Lerner's "underground mentality" was still preventing her from either joining the Communist Party or taking public political action. She continued working as an X-ray technician at the same time that she improved her language skills and her confidence by writing stories in English that were getting published. However, by 1946 several developments motivated Lerner finally to join the Communist Party and become a public activist.

First were the courses in writing and literature she took in Hollywood with John Howard Lawson, later called the "Communist cultural czar of Hollywood" by the House Un-American Activities Committee (HUAC). In Lawson's courses, Lerner studied how race, class, and gender operated as interconnected oppressions throughout American history.[73]

The connections Lawson drew between women's suffrage and the labor movement must undoubtedly have contributed to Lerner's volunteering for Franklin Delano Roosevelt's 1944 campaign for president, even while she was still working full-time. This second step toward greater political activism exposed her directly to gender and class divisions in the campaign. She remarked that in the leafletting, house visits, and voter registration drives she supervised as a "precinct captain" for the Democratic Party, she first observed gender/class divisions that would recur in succeeding election campaigns in California and New York: Volunteers like herself were mostly women, but staff members were men.[74]

She brought this awareness of the connection between women's unpaid work and the more general exploitation of labor into her work for the Congress of American Women (CAW), which she joined in October 1946. She helped to found two chapters, in Los Angeles and Hollywood, at the time when women were organizing boycotts against the dramatic rise in meat prices after World War II.

CAW was the United States branch of the Women's International Democratic Federation (WIDF), an international organization representing 81 million women from forty countries. WIDF was devoted to advancing women's rights, to protecting children, and to striving for world peace and democracy. Lerner, who by this time had a daughter with Carl, had three main concerns: the right of workers, including those like Carl in the film industry, to unionize; the fight against racism; and resistance to nuclear weapons and war in order to protect children and succeeding generations. The latter issue catapulted her out of her underground mentality.[75]

Earlier, in August 1945, when then-President Truman called for the atomic bombing of Japan with the rationale to end the war and save American lives, Lerner's personal history as a Jewish refugee compelled her to become more politically visible and to emphasize race more fully into her analysis of oppression in the United States. Her analysis had already accounted for gender and class. "Saving the lives of U.S. soldiers in exchange for killing a hundred and sixty thousand Japanese civilians was close to the 'reasoning' of the Nazi regime and its concept of the superiority of the German 'race.'" This was "the kind of thinking that had made fascism possible." Lerner became an avid peace activist and began to live in the United States "in opposition to government policy."[76]

Government policy at this time included the strong anti-Soviet sentiment that mushroomed into Cold War politics. The reasoning that Lerner called "the big lie" was that socialism in any form was seditious and un-American.[77] Lerner knew it was a lie because, like so many others whom she knew in Hollywood—a primary location targeted by Communist witch hunts—she joined the Communist Party and endorsed socialism not to destabilize democracy but to make it stronger. It was the Communists Lerner knew who were "stronger, more consistent fighters" than anyone else for decent housing, consumer price controls, workers' rights, and adequate childcare.[78] But in the anti-Soviet climate that inundated the country shortly after the end of the war, Communists were suspect:

> All American Communists and their sympathizers and defenders were involved in an evil conspiracy to overthrow democratic government. . . . Guilt by association was an accepted fact. . . . If they acted like Communists . . . they were Communists. . . . And Communists had become the devil, the witches, the traitors.[79]

Simply put, the Communist witch hunts triggered for Lerner a repeat of her experience being a Jew vulnerable to genocide under fascism. She had walked the swastika-plastered streets of Vienna and had seen wall newspapers containing cartoons of "ugly old Jews in kaftans and stiff hats, hook-nosed with bulging lips," the way no real Jew ever looked. But "the idea was to fix the image in the mind of the beholder until he could superimpose it on reality" so that it would *substitute* for reality.[80]

Looking back on the 1930s of her adolescence, she wrote from her vantage point in late 1940s America:

> Now I walked through American streets . . . and the headlines screaming at me from the newsstands seemed exactly as they had been then. Now the Communist devil was incarnate, the outcast, the deviant. . . . Escape, we had dreamed in Vienna. America . . . Now I was in America and there was no escape.[81]

The inevitable parallels Lerner drew between the United States' attempt to rout out Communists and the Nazis' attempt to rout out first Communists and then Jews became most palpable for her when Carl Lerner was blacklisted as a Communist because of his union activism.[82] Not able to get hired any longer in Hollywood, Carl took a chance in February 1949 to rebuild his career in TV and film alone in New York where a friend promised him work. Meanwhile, Lerner, who by now had two young children, was once again realizing how it felt to be targeted by the politics of fear-mongering, being labeled and stigmatized as one of the "deviant outgroups" on the blacklist.[83] She felt especially vulnerable caring for her family on her own in California without Carl and without financial security.

In that same year, 1949, Lerner came to see the Soviet Union to be as much of a threat to world security as the United States. The Soviets exploded their first atomic weapons.

> I was motivated by a simple and primitive sense of danger to my own child and the world's children, and by the emotional resonance of my experiences with the coming of fascism.[84]

Once the Soviets exhibited nuclear capability, the Cold War intensified under President Truman. However, Lerner's disenchantment with the Soviets did not extend to her feelings about Communism, which she continued to support. The U.S. government, on the other hand, conflated Communism with the Soviets. Anyone supporting nuclear disarmament in the U.S., which would weaken the country in a time of cold war, was no doubt a pawn of the Soviets. Lerner's main political activity in 1949, as a member of CAW's national board, became circulating the Stockholm Appeal demanding nuclear disarmament around the world. The U.S. government and the media denounced the Appeal as a tool of Communist propaganda.[85] The government challenge to CAW was so destructive that the organization chose to disband in 1950 rather than spend time in a lawsuit bound to be unsuccessful. Was the Soviet Union really going to wage nuclear war against the U.S. after having lost 22 million people in World War II? The Cold War fomented this fear and labeled supporters of world peace as Communist traitors, using blacklists, firings, imprisonments, and deportations as means of quelling dissent.

The deportations struck closest to home with Lerner, sounding echoes of her experiences in fascist Austria. The nightmares still inhabiting her "underground mentality" were becoming tragic realities. Organizations for which she was writing and advocating were all included as subversive under the Internal Security Act of 1950. They were considered Communist-front organizations, the members of which were prohibited from holding government office, working in a defense plant, or applying for, using, or attempting to use a passport.[86]

The Kilgore Concentration Camp provision of that same act allowed for the arrest and detention of persons about whom there was "reasonable ground to believe" they would "engage in an act of espionage or sabotage."[87] A person could be denied a passport or sent to a detention camp without evidence of any criminality—just the *belief* that this person would *probably* conspire unpatriotically. No more due process, no more presumption of innocence until proven guilty. "It was not dissimilar," Lerner wrote, "to the state of existence I had experienced in Vienna after the *Anschluss* [the Nazi takeover of Austria]. . . . One lived in constant anxiety, as though under a suspended sword, waiting for the blade to fall. . . . I identified with each and every . . . one" of the "potential deportees. There but for the grace of God go I."[88]

Why did Lerner, a nonobservant, secular Jew, use God-language to articulate her fears of deportation? In *Fireweed*, she even calls herself an agnostic.[89] In calling out to God, Lerner demonstrates a common pattern among Jewish skeptics of religious faith and even of God's existence.

She expresses herself, even her doubts, from the insider position of her Jewishness.[90]

It was the Rosenberg case—the executions of Julius and Ethel Rosenberg, accused of being Soviet spies and convicted without any hard evidence of espionage—that brought Lerner closest in her writing to the God about whose existence she had no certainty.

Lerner was an activist in the defense of the Rosenbergs and was at the death vigil in Union Square the night of the executions, June 20, 1953. She wrote that she felt she had lost a member of her own family.[91] The case reminded her of the 1933 Reichstag bombing in Berlin that had been pinned on a mentally retarded Dutch citizen who, ostensibly, had been put up to it by a Bulgarian Communist. Though the Dutch citizen ultimately was proven innocent, his being framed by the Nazis had the desired effect of proving to the German people that Communists were indeed a threat to Germany. Likewise, in the Rosenberg case, insufficient evidence was being marshaled to affirm an unwarranted execution in order to prove to the United States' population that the search for Communist traitors on the part of police, FBI, and congressional and state committees was justified. Investigations that had begun in the late 1940s had not yet yielded even one conviction.[92]

The death penalty seemed overly severe, even to those who believed that the Rosenbergs were guilty of conspiracy. Lerner explained that "many Jews believed the Rosenbergs were treated so harshly because they were Jews," since "no civilian had ever been executed in the U.S.A. for either spying or treason." It was believed there was a subtext behind the conviction which was "to prove what all the previous persecutions and hearings had been unable to prove, that Communists were traitors and spies. Especially Jewish ones."[93]

In the time shortly following the executions, while Lerner was driving somewhere with her two children, she overheard on the car radio that one of her own doctors in Los Angeles had become an informer. Convinced by this of the total breakdown of all honor, trust, and friendship, she became terrified because of her own Communist affiliation. For another rare instant in her writing, Lerner acknowledged feeling that only a power beyond her control could possibly save her family from the kind of utter ruin that had befallen the Rosenbergs' sons, and she resorted to prayer: "Above all, I *prayed*, let me be strong enough to keep dailiness going. Let me save these children from troubled waters."[94] To whom did she pray? To a God whose existence was not part of her belief?

Historian of Women

In 1958, Lerner enrolled in the New School of Social Research to learn the history that would enable her to complete a novel she was writing on the Grimké sisters, the only daughters of slave-holding plantation owners to become anti-slavery agents in the north and pioneers for women's rights. Her creative writing career—with short stories, novels, theatrical productions, and films under her belt, all on political subjects dealing with race, gender, and class—was being stymied by the anti-Communist climate.[95]

Yet how could she abandon writing about race, gender, and class, the very issues to which she was committed as an activist? These were the same issues of her concern, as we have seen, throughout her adolescence in Austria, her years as wartime and postwar refugee, and her life as a left-wing radical in the United States. She had to find ways to continue writing about these important markers of identity. At the conclusion of *Fireweed*, she explained that these were markers of her identity as well. These "convictions" of hers, she wrote, were rooted in her own experience "as an anti-fascist, as a Jew, as an unskilled immigrant worker, and as a woman."[96]

Lerner decided that if it would be too difficult to publish fiction about the operation of gender, race, and class throughout the lives of women in the United States, then it would be better to write and publish about these issues in the field of history, where they could be canonized in the historical record. She forged ahead, majoring in history at the New School with the goal of focusing on women.

The Grimké novel ultimately became the dissertation she wrote for her doctoral degree in history at Columbia, where she earned both an MA and a PhD. She transformed the dissertation into her first scholarly book publication, *The Grimké Sisters from South Carolina* (1967), and followed that with the article "The Lady and the Mill Girl" (1969) about class differences among women in the United States in the Jacksonian era.[97]

Then she published *Black Women in White America* (1972), a documentary anthology that proved to doubters that the field of Black Women's History did indeed exist.

When the mother-in-law of Lerner's friend and neighbor Sarah, who was Black, questioned Lerner about her choice to live and raise her family in the interracial neighborhood of St. Albans, Queens, Lerner gave her clearest, most concise summary of her connection as a Jew to the plight of Blacks in the United States. The dialogue between Lerner and Sarah's mother-in-law is worthy of inclusion here:

> "It's because we're Jewish. And I, in particular, am a refugee from Hitler."
>
> "Yeah, Sarah told me that. I'm sorry to hear that. I haven't had much contact with Jewish people. So I can't understand—"
>
> "You've lived in the Jim Crow South. You've been excluded from public rest rooms, restaurants, trains. Segregated because of race. Well, after Hitler came, Jews in Vienna were not only excluded from schools, public places, parks, but fired from their jobs, imprisoned without cause, many sent to concentration camps. And as you know, six million were killed, deliberately, men, women, and children. So to me, any kind of discrimination is evil. I can't stand it. I want my children free of it."[98]

In 1979, Lerner published *The Majority Finds Its Past*, the collection of her essays that examine women's differences in American history across class, ethnicity, race, and culture. Then in 1987, she published a sweeping, epic treatment of women's exclusion from Western history since ancient times, *The Creation of Patriarchy*. This work addresses elements of the Hebrew Bible directly. It analyzes the depictions of God, the creation of humanity and succeeding generations, and the role of circumcision in the covenant to show that the ideas, symbols, and metaphors of the Hebrew Bible transform the goddess worship of the ancient world into a basically masculine concept of deity, lineage, and communal responsibility.[99]

In the period during 1991–93, Lerner felt called upon again to explore her "relationship with the fact of being Jewish" when "the agony of the state of Israel" was in the public eye. The "agony" to which she referred, commonly known as the first *intifada*, was the Palestinian uprising against the Israeli occupation of the West Bank and Gaza. Lerner had never been an ardent Zionist, since she feared the dangerous consequences of extreme nationalism:

> Coming out of my own experience of fascism, I had become convinced that nationalism of any kind could only lead to conflict and war. . . . I wanted to get away from nationalistic allegiances; I wanted to transcend differences of race, ethnicity, religion and nationality. I saw my choice as "either-or."[100]

But the Israeli-Palestinian controversy, and subsequent criticisms of Israel, led her to rethink her understanding of Israel's significance, even to a nonreligious, secular Jew like herself. She understood that Israel means "the first time in two thousand years Jews no longer . . . allow themselves to be defined by others who scapegoated them." Such group self-definition is commonly affirmed as "self-determination and freedom." Having a national home in Israel can mean having reprieve from living "from pogrom to pogrom" if one is Jewish. It can mean not having to look over one's shoulder with one's "bags packed."[101]

Nevertheless, Lerner believed the Israeli conflict between Jews and Arabs illustrated, even more importantly than Jewish self-determination, the greater essential lesson of universalism, that the world no longer needs a focus on "the small group, the kin, the shtetl, the *Landsmannshaft*, even the nation." Her own history of suffering as a Jew, an outsider, and an "other" taught her that stressing one group's autonomy above another's has led historically to domination and oppression. What we need to survive is mutual respect for and celebration of our differences:

> All of us must survive in a world in which difference is the norm and no longer serves as an excuse for dominance, or we will not survive at all. And in order to survive in this interconnected global village we must learn and learn very quickly to respect others who are different from us and, ultimately, to grant others the autonomy we demand for ourselves. In short, celebrate difference and banish hatred.[102]

In summary, Lerner gleaned important lessons from years of scholarly research and experience as an activist living through the Holocaust and the Cold War. She saw that the differences that distinguish and divide people can offer comfort and security in times when individual and group survival is being threatened. But she also saw that the powerful can ultimately manipulate the less powerful by using racial, ethnic, national, economic, and gender differences in ways that control and oppress. She believed that the human community must find a path toward inter-group peace and survival, without allowing one religious, cultural, economic, national, or ethnic group to dominate another.

Nevertheless, we can ask: In her work of fostering bonds and under-standings among people across lines of gender, class, and race, did she erase her Jewish identity or impede Jewish continuity? We have seen how she viewed the universalism of her scholarly and activist work as emerging from Jewish values. We may agree that Lerner could say, along with Mark Hetfield, president of HIAS, that she devoted her effort to the repair of the world *because* she was Jewish.

Yet, during her career as an academic historian, colleagues did ques-tion why she didn't write specifically about Jewish women or her own Jewish identity until the 1990s. She was, after all, a Holocaust survivor sensitive to oppression based on anti-Semitism. Why didn't she affiliate as a member of the Association for Jewish Studies or with the Jewish Caucus of the National Women's Studies Association, since these inter-disciplinary fields were burgeoning around her? With her chosen field as Women's History, she affiliated instead with nondenominational orga-nizations of historians, the American Historical Association, the Berk-shire Women's History Conference, and the Organization of American Historians, where she served as president in 1980–81.

Lerner was aware that there were Jewish-affiliated lacunae in her profile, and she seems to address them, if only indirectly, in the intro-duction to *Fireweed: A Political Autobiography*, which appeared in 2002:

> In the past decades I have been frequently interviewed and ques-tioned about my life and my development as a historian. . . . But I have been silent about my political past during the years of my academic success. And such silence, for all its complex reasons, distorts the truth. Now I would like to set the record straight. That is why I have written a "political," and "partial" autobiography to

explain the roads I have taken, the world in which I lived, the choices I have made in the world. . . . I do not want to end my life within a closet of my own making.[103]

However, the autobiography does not address her lack of scholarly writing on Jewish issues. The only place I have found Lerner raising the question directly of why she never focused on *Jewish* women in her scholarship is in her earlier essay "A Weave of Connections." After explaining that as an American, she wanted to write about the most important racism facing the country, that being discrimination against American Blacks, she then asserts that for her to focus on Jewish women would somehow be like her endorsing a kind of nationalism: "I wanted to get away from nationalistic allegiances; I wanted to transcend differences of race, ethnicity, religion and nationality."[104] But clearly she was not transcending ethnicity and race by focusing on American Blacks. She was, however, transcending her own ethnicity and religion by avoiding a focus on identity politics that she may have found too limiting and narrow, given her global vision of world peace.

In the same essay, she admits that at one time she upheld her mother's assimilationist philosophy that we could, as a human community, find "tolerance and a 'new humanism'" if we gave up all distinctiveness in order "to embrace different cultures, religions and nationalities." But Lerner closes her essay, as we have seen, on an entirely different note, by appealing to our need to celebrate rather than shed our differences: "All of us *must* . . . celebrate difference and banish hatred."[105] Fervently Lerner wished for us to reach this goal.

How then shall we understand more fully what lay behind her late-life need finally to review her own feelings of difference as a Jew and a woman, her need to write and share her Jewish personal history in *Fireweed* and in the articles of the 1990s that preceded it? Had she realized that she had been sublimating repressed guilt about her past as a Jew—abandoning her mother in Europe and focusing on her new life in America instead—by choosing to write about other marginalized groups and not about Jews? Would writing about Jewish women have brought her too close to the mental anguish she never expressed until later in her scholarly career? Did she need distance from her past in order to empathize as fully as she did with other subjugated groups of women?

On the other hand, if we take Lerner at her word, her rejection of a focus on Jewish women may have ultimately resulted from "a complex weave of connections."[106] That weave simultaneously included viewing identity politics as too restrictive, given her global concerns, and her resistance to revisiting fears and wounds of the underground mentality which continued to haunt her, but which she finally exposed and reckoned with in the last decades of her life.

While Gerda Lerner may not have made her Jewishness prominent during her career, Jewishness is nevertheless everywhere evident in her dominant scholarly theme: No persons or women should ever be made into "others" the way Jews were made into "others" by fascism during the Holocaust. By pursuing this theme, Lerner became a major founder of the fields of Women's History in general and of Black Women's History in particular. In addition, her multilayered approach to identity, incorporating race, gender, and class, is nothing short of a forerunner of today's "intersectionality,"[107] the dominant feminist theory of identity that helps us broaden our grasp of who we are as complex beings in the world.

Eventually Lerner did bring her attention as a scholar with an intersectional approach to Jewish women, seeing how the complexity of Jewish women's identities in terms of class, race, gender, and sexuality contributed to the fabric of American history. She avidly supported the Jewish Women's Archive and became a member of its Academic Advisory Council.[108]

Notes

1. Gerda Lerner, *Black Women in White America* (New York: Pantheon, 1972).
2. Radical feminists were uncovering the false presentation of women as subordinate "others" in contrast to the presentation of males as the norm. Texts that have become classics include Kate Millet's *Sexual Politics* (New York: Columbia University Press, 1969); Shulamith Firestone's *The Dialectics of Sex* (New York: William Morrow & Co., 1970), and Susan Brownmiller's *Against Our Will* (New York: Simon and Schuster, 1975). Radical

feminists pointed to patriarchal gender relations as the root cause of women's oppression.

3. In addition to *Black Women in White America,* many of Lerner's other scholarly works emphasize women's agency, including *The Grimké Sisters of South Carolina* (New York: Houghton Mifflin, 1967); *The Majority Finds Its Past* (New York: Oxford University Press, 1979); *The Creation of Feminist Consciousness* (New York: Oxford University Press, 1993), and *Why History Matters* (New York: Oxford University Press, 1997).

4. Joyce Antler, "Remembering Gerda Lerner: The 'Mother' of Women's History," January 13, 2013, *Jewish Women's Archive;* https://jwa.org/blog/remembering-gerda-lerner-mother-of-womens-history.

5. In 2014 I organized a panel for the 46th Annual Association for Jewish Studies to honor Gerda Lerner's legacy as a Jewish feminist historian and her contributions to women's history— "Interdisciplinary Approaches to Jewish Identity: What Counts as 'Jewish' in Our Scholarship and in the Pioneering Work of Feminist Historian Gerda Lerner" (December 14–16, 2014, Hilton Hotel Baltimore, Maryland). In the discussion that followed, Lerner was criticized for not belonging to the Association for Jewish Studies. Her non-affiliation, it was said, did damage to the Jewish women who were attempting to provide a feminist presence within the association. In the field of Black Women's History, Lerner's book is sometimes not included in lists of the foundational texts, like John H. Bracey Jr.'s 1986 list, for example, in "Afro-American Women: A Brief Guide to Writings from Historical and Feminist Perspectives," *Contributions in Black Studies: A Journal of African and Afro-American Studies:* Vol 8, Article 9. Available at: http://scholarworks.umass.edu/cibs/vol8/iss1/9. It may be that some Black scholars are cautious not to usurp the role of leading Black feminist scholars of Black Women's History, such as Rosalyn Terborg-Penn and Darlene Clark-Hine, by identifying the importance of Gerda Lerner's trailblazing research.

6. Jerald E. Podair, *The Strike That Changed New York: Blacks, Whites, and the Ocean Hill-Brownsville Crisis* (New Haven: Yale University Press, 2002), 48–70.

7. http://originalpeople.org/new-york-city-teachers-strike-of-1968-blacks-and-jews-battle-over-control-of-black-school-district (posted November 15, 2012).

8. Podair, 1–8.

9. Lerner, *Fireweed : A Political Autobiography* (Philadelphia: Temple University Press, 2002), 158–59. For information on Gerda Lerner's life, I rely heavily on my close reading of *Fireweed*, and on the essay "A Weave of Connections" in *Why History Matters*, 3–17.

10. Lerner, *Fireweed*, 45–47, 50–52.

11. Lerner, "A Weave of Connections," *Why History Matters*, 16.

12. Ibid., 5. Joyce Antler, "History and Gender," *Frontiers: A Journal of Women's Studies*, Vol. 36, No. 1 (2015), 16–21. Also Joyce Antler "Remembering Gerda Lerner: The 'Mother' of Women's History."

13. Lerner, "A Weave of Connections," *Why History Matters*, 16.

14. Ibid., 3.

15. Lerner, *Fireweed*, 39.

16. Ibid., 40–41, 44.

17. Ibid., 40.

18. Lerner, "The Covenant," *The Creation of Patriarchy* (New York: Oxford University Press, 1986), 188–93.

19. Lerner, "A Weave of Connections," *Why History Matters*, 6.

20. Ibid., 7.

21. Ibid., 4–5. See also Lerner, *Fireweed*, 35–42.

22. Lerner, *Fireweed*, 40.

23. Ibid., 58–60.

24. Ibid., 20.

25. Ibid., 22.

26. Ibid., 44.

27. Ibid., 48.

28. Ibid., 44.

29. Ibid., 58–59.

30. Ibid., 46.

31. Ibid., 44.

32. Ibid., 23–24, 36–37.

33. Ibid., 23.

34. Ibid., 36, 40–41.

35. Ibid., 42.

36. Ibid., 55, 61–65, 68–69.

37. Ibid., 55.

38. Ibid., 84.

39. Ibid., 92, 118.

40. Ibid., 83–84

41. Ibid., 121.

42. Ibid., 85–86.

43. Ibid., 86–91.

44. Ibid., 94–95.

45. Ibid., 115.

46. Ibid., 106.

47. Ibid., 105.

48. Ibid., 122.

49. Ibid., 119.

50. Ibid., 122.

51. https://www.ushmm.org/wlc/en/article.php?ModuleId=10005201.

52. Lerner, *Fireweed*, 124–25.

53. Ibid., 135, 141, 147.

54. Ibid., 139.

55. Ibid., 137–40.

56. Ibid., 162–63.

57. Ibid., 170–81, 193–200, 204–07.

58. Ibid., 170.

59. Ibid., 179, 181.

60. Ibid., 179.

61. Ibid., 160–62.

62. Ibid., 178–80, 193–99, 250–51, 292.

63. Ibid., 157–58, 166, 180–81.

64. Ibid., 156.

65. Ibid., 191, 228.

66. Ibid., 208–09.

67. Ibid., 208.

68. Ibid., 224.

69. Ibid., 191–92.

70. Lerner, "A Weave of Connections," 5–7.

71. Lerner, *Fireweed*, 190.

72. Ibid., 224.

73. Ibid., 233–34.

74. Ibid., 236.

75. Ibid., 243–49, 252–55.

76. Ibid., 244–45.

77. Ibid., 224.

78. Ibid., 255.

79. Ibid., 297.

80. Ibid., 297–98.

81. Ibid., 298–99.

82. Ibid., 294–95.

83. Ibid., 300.

84. Ibid., 245.

85. Ibid., 272–74.

86. Ibid., 325.

87. Ibid.

88. Ibid., 326–28.

89. Ibid., 42.

90. The tradition in Jewish literature of criticizing God and challenging God's existence from the "insider" position of Jewish identity can be traced to biblical works, such as the Book of Job. See also Note 94.

91. Lerner, *Fireweed*, 333.

92. Ibid., 330–31.

93. Ibid., 329–31.

94. Ibid., 334–35, italics added. Lerner's pleas to God to enable her to protect her children contain echoes of Elie Wiesel's often-quoted lines from his Holocaust memoir *Night* (New York: Hill and Wang, 1960), chapter 6, paragraph 65: "And in spite of myself, a prayer formed inside me, a prayer to this God in whom I no longer believed."

95. Ibid., 365–67.

96. Ibid., 369.

97. Gerda Lerner, "The Lady and the Mill Girl," *American Studies Journal*, Vol. 10, No. 1, spring 1969, 5–15. See also Note 3.

98. Lerner, *Fireweed*, 322.

99. See Notes 3 and 18.

100. Lerner, "A Weave of Connections," 16.

101. Ibid., 15.

102. Ibid., 17.

103. Lerner, *Fireweed*, 3.

104. Lerner, "A Weave of Connections," 16.

105. Ibid., 13, 17, italics added.

106. Ibid., 16.

107. The term was coined by legal scholar Kimberlé Crenshaw in a 1989 essay, "Demarginalizing the Intersection of Race and Sex: A Black Feminist Critique of Antidiscrimination Doctrine, Feminist Theory, and Antiracist Politics," *University of Chicago Legal Forum*, 1989, 139–67. Crenshaw asserts that anti-discrimination law, feminist theory, and antiracist politics all fail to address the experiences of Black women because of how they each focus on only a single factor. Crenshaw writes that "because the intersectional experience is greater than the sum of racism and sexism, any analysis that does not take intersectionality into account cannot sufficiently address the particular manner in which Black women are subordinated." Though originally applied only to the ways that sexism and racism combine and overlap, *intersectionality* has come to include other forms of discrimination as well, such as those based on class, sexuality, and ability; https://www.merriam-webster.com/words-at-play/intersectionality-meaning.

108. Antler, "History and Gender," 20–21.

2

SUSANA WALD (1937–)

Personal Association

I was able to befriend the feminist Surrealist artist and writer Susana Wald in 2007 when I was spending winters in the city of Oaxaca, Mexico. A Chilean-Canadian, Wald resided in Oaxaca beginning in 1994 with her colleague and life partner, the poet Ludwig Zeller (1927–2019). Since Zeller's death, she has been dividing her time between Toronto, Canada and Oaxaca.

Studying Wald's life, I became familiar not only with Jewish aspects of Surrealism, but also with Surrealism in South America, about which texts in English are few. English-speaking audiences have become more aware of Wald's reputation internationally as feminist art historians begin to link Wald to other Surrealist women artists such as Leonora Carrington and Remedios Varo, both of whom, like Wald, were born elsewhere but worked in Mexico.[1]

Before I met Susana Wald, a mutual friend told me that Wald was a Jewish survivor of the Holocaust from Budapest, Hungary, and that she had been saved by the famous Swedish rescuer Raoul Wallenberg. I also knew that Wald had declared herself publicly to be Jewish in 2006 when, at age seventy-six, she was asked to speak at a rally in Oaxaca during the mass uprising against the government that had captured international attention.[2] It was the first time she had presented herself as Jewish to the community-at-large.

I was eager to meet Wald because I had been a teacher of Holocaust literature and was continuing to write about trauma and memory.[3]

However, I had not yet connected the Holocaust and memory to Surrealism, and I began to ponder the subject. Had Wald, a lifelong artist, been completely silent about her Jewish identity before her residence in Oaxaca, I wondered, and what was it about the uprising that prompted her to pronounce herself as Jewish?

Six years after I met Wald, I began interviewing her.[4] I learned that, although she began her life as a deeply spiritual person, she felt compelled during most of her years to keep her Jewish identity undercover. Even so, she began entering the political arena as an artist in 1963 shortly after meeting Zeller in Chile. Together they practiced Surrealism, employing their art and writing as vehicles for changing social consciousness. Living as a Surrealist changed Wald's life radically.

During Salvador Allende's fourth bid to gain the Chilean presidency in 1970, Wald and Zeller organized the exhibition "Surrealism in Chile" at Universidad Católica de Chile. In that show, which received full-page coverage in an important daily, Wald and Zeller hung a provocative, humorously political mannequin named "Presidenciable" from the ceiling of the exhibit hall as if it were a presidential candidate. The exhibition was just one of many events known as "happenings" that Zeller and Wald sponsored in Santiago through the independent cultural center they founded, Casa de la Luna (1968). Needless to say, the exhibition, along with previous "happenings," marked Wald and Zeller as "shit disturbers," a term Wald applied at times to herself alone.[5]

These activities preceded their abrupt flight from Santiago to Toronto, Canada, shortly after Allende's inauguration as president in November 1970. Immediately after the inauguration, they experienced negative political consequences. They feared their situation would become worse during the right-wing military coup that was rumored to erupt in the radicalized and violent atmosphere surrounding Allende's presidency. Once in Toronto, Wald lived and worked as a Surrealist artist, teacher, and writer, becoming known internationally. In 1994 her long-term residence in Oaxaca began. Despite recognition as an artist, Wald did not feel safe "coming out" as Jewish until later in her life.[6] I needed to more fully understand why.

When I first met Wald and Zeller in their home in Oaxaca, I was accompanied by my husband, Milton. Wald gravitated to us, desired to be in our company, and said how much Milton and I, both of us from Eastern European Jewish roots, reminded her of her Jewish origins. In Wald's memoir, *Life Matters: Windows*, she describes her memories of our time together:

> As we begin to eat Milton quietly mentions that this is a Sabbath meal. Yes, I say, the Sabbath has just begun a few minutes ago. This becomes our victory night in memory of the big genocide against our people. They wanted to eliminate us from the face of the Earth, it didn't work, Wallenberg intervened. I'm alive. I feel great joy . . . Victories don't always happen on battlefields. Life matters.[7]

For ten years, Wald would participate in a writing group that I led, where she shared segments of her as yet unpublished memoir, written according to many of the principles of Surrealism.[8]

From this memoir, my interviews with her, and from books and articles by and about her, I learned of her extraordinary achievements as an artist, author, and translator whose creative works span many traditional and innovative genres.[9] She was also kind and gracious enough to trust me with details of her life that went beyond professional accomplishments. Most importantly for this study, she disclosed information about the arc of her Jewish experience, the relationships she forged between Surrealism and Jewish identity, and the particular decision points in time when she was driven to abandon protective covers and to respond directly as a Jew.

Professional Accomplishments

Wald's accomplishments are impressive. Her work in writing includes editing, journalism, translation, and language texts. She is author of the original *Spanish for Dummies*.[10] She also writes in innovative literary forms. Her memoir, *Life Matters: Windows*, for example, is a collage of vignettes she began writing in her seventies. The vignettes link repetitive images, such as rooms, windows, and eyes, which move hauntingly through time and memory as in dreams. Like other well-known Surrealists, Wald mines dreams as rich resources for her creative expression, attempting in part to obliterate linear social constructs such as time.[11]

Mural Mandrágora, Talca, Chile

Wald's artwork is visual, plastic, and literary. Her visual and plastic art includes drawing, painting, sculpture, and public murals. Her literary art includes the publication, design, and illustration of books, magazines, and newspapers.[12]

Wald's paintings have been recognized internationally in the prestigious Venice Biennial (1986) and the UNESCO Traveling Show Iberoamerica Pinta (1997–2000). Her murals are on display in Talca, Chile; Toronto, Canada; and Tiripetio, Michoacan, in Mexico.[13]

Wald also created a unique form called "collaborative mirages" with her artistic partner Ludwig Zeller. These are collages by Zeller accompanied by drawing and painting by Wald. A noteworthy example is the one-of-a-kind book in French that Wald and Zeller published of André Breton's poem "Vigilance." Breton is founder of Surrealism, and this text presents Wald's specially handwritten, calligraphic version of Breton's poem, set amidst the highly original "mirages" she and Zeller designed together. In addition, Wald co-arranged the various artistic "happenings" at Casa de la Luna and other cultural settings that identified her and Zeller as social critics.[14]

With artworks exhibited internationally in solo and group shows and owned by many private and public collections, and with various forms of written work and literary art, Wald is one of the leading women responsible for shepherding the main tenets of Surrealism—Freedom, Creativity, Love—into the twenty-first century.[15]

A Threatened Jewish Core, a Miraculous Rescue

As a Jew growing up in war-torn Hungary of the late 1930s and 1940s, where the seeds of fascism were already sown by worldwide depression and the rise of ultra-nationalism, Wald felt marked as an "outsider" and lived in constant fear. She described the broad sweep of this feeling in the epigraph to the 2003 book about her life and art, *Susana Wald*: "It is a condition of my life that I have been an outsider everywhere, even in Budapest, the city where I was born."[16]

That Wald applied the "outsider" motif to her entire life is significant, since the Jew has represented the outsider in Western art and literature for centuries. Since ancient times, the Hebrew has been conflated with the "other," the stranger, as in Exodus.[17] In 2013, when Rabbi David Meyer testified before the United States House Foreign Affairs and Human Rights subcommittee on the status of anti-Semitism in Europe, he observed that "even after 2,000 years we [Jews] are still perceived as a foreign tribe newly landed on the Continent."[18] Wald's self-identification as an outsider therefore links her to the Western narrative about Jews, though Wald's sense of marginalization is amplified further by her being a woman as well as an artist.

Even so, the young Wald developed a strong, positive sense of Jewish identity both culturally and spiritually in 1940s Budapest, despite threats to her and her family's survival because they were Jews. Her Jewish *cultural* identity, deriving from family traditions and parental values, provided her with a sense of belonging to the Jewish people, *am yisroel*, her ethnic group.[19] Her *spiritual* identity as a Jew grew, on the other hand, from her personal need to nurture an inner self, a self that could respond to the world around her with a child's sense of awe and wonder despite the terrifying brutality of her surroundings. Wald's deeply spiritual nature gave rise to her creative imagination, at the same time that its Jewish origins required constant, vigilant protection. She experienced her Jewish spiritual center as the most precious and endangered part of her being.

Wald was born into a family of Jewish identity and heritage, well integrated into dominant Hungarian society. Wald's father, George, was a successful traveling salesman for Palma, a large rubber manufacturing firm. Her mother, Ibolya (Violet), a stunningly attractive woman who appeared non-Jewish, had been a concertizing pianist who studied with Béla Bartók at the musical academy of Budapest. The Walds were Hungarian-speaking, while also fluent in German like many Hungarian families. With nostalgia, they spoke fondly of Hungary as their homeland, though conditions after the war forced them to leave and to find greater security in Argentina.[20]

By contrast, Wald told her biographer, Martha Mabey, that she considered *her* "homeland" to be her "*inner* world" because of the many "wars, revolutions, exiles and physical dislocations" she had lived through. At different points in her life, she referred to her inner world as an entity that must remain inviolate, untouched by any worldly turbulence. She named it in psycho-spiritual and universal terms as "psyche, soul, the unconscious, and even the voice of God."[21]

The original voice of God Wald heard was shaped by her Jewish upbringing in Budapest where she knew, noncognitively as a young child, that being Jewish was noble and important, but also life-threatening. She distinctly recalls certain spiritual/cultural imagery and sensory impressions of Jewish life observed in her family before the Nazis occupied Hungary in March 1944. Those images and sounds include traditional observances, though the Walds were mainly nonobservant.[22]

Wald recalls her mother, Ibolya, as "religious" in her own way, performing Jewish rituals like lighting memorial candles at home for loved ones who died and fasting during Yom Kippur, the Day of Atonement. She recalls her father, George, as always "certain of being a Jew." He was born a Kohein, a member of the Jewish priestly class descended from Aaron, the brother of Moses. Though George held atheistic and agnostic ideas, he read in Hebrew from the Torah in the synagogue while the young Wald sat with her paternal female relatives on the second floor in the area designated for women. Even after George emigrated with his family to Argentina in 1949 to escape Joseph Stalin's rule over Hungary, Wald remembers him never abandoning his attachment to Jewish identity.[23]

But these memories were overrun in Wald's mind as a child by unsettling fears whenever her parents and extended family talked nervously about persecutions of Jews, the takeover of Austria in 1938, and the beginning of war in 1939. At the Friday afternoon and evening family gatherings in the Budapest home of Mathilde Frank, Wald's maternal grandmother, Wald and her young cousins overheard their relatives' concerns as they anxiously discussed each newly posted restriction on Jews. As in the Vienna experienced by Gerda Lerner, so in the Budapest of Wald's family, posters were hung in public locations where Jews could read about newly imposed restrictions. Wald's family joked, "Is this good for us?" and they pondered whether anything could be done about each new law and the degree to which this or that would ultimately be detrimental for the Jews.[24]

Under Regent Miklós Horthy, the Hungarian government issued the First Jewish Law in 1935, two years before Wald was born. The law limited the percentage of Jews who could practice different professions. The Second Jewish Law of 1939, defining Jews as a race, not just a religion, set a national policy of forced Jewish emigration.[25]

When Wald was a toddler, waves of mass deportations and killings throughout the Hungarian countryside caused a storm cloud of fear and worry to hover over the family members gathered at Grandmother Frank's home at 26 Damjanics Street. The Walds sensed it was just a matter of time before the Jews of Budapest would become targets.[26]

Wald would be reminded of this time of worry she experienced as a young child sixteen years later in Buenos Aires when she met José Hausner, who became her first husband. Hausner's family perished in Auschwitz after having been deported from the Hungarian countryside. Recollections of this common history bonded them.[27]

In January 1942, atrocities struck Novi Sad, then part of Hungary's southern region and the birthplace of Wald's Grandmother Frank. Hungarian troops in collaboration with the Axis powers massacred over three thousand men, women, and children in Novi Sad, a third of them Jews, under pretext of their Partisan resistance activities. None of the Franks living in that city survived.[28]

Becoming more and more distressed by news of these worsening conditions, the Walds couldn't help but ask themselves again how long it would be before mass killings and deportations would reach Budapest. They told jokes to ease their tensions and huddled together to enjoy humorous stories, some by their neighbor Frigyes Karinthy, the well-known satirist who lived across the way at number 24 and whose family had originally been Jewish. By contrast, the Walds held fast to their identity as Jews, even while conditions increasingly marked and targeted them as part of the unwanted "race."[29]

The turning point came sometime between 1939 and 1940 when Wald's father and maternal uncle were conscripted—because they were Jews—into hard labor with the Jewish Labor Service, *munkaszolgalat*, an *unarmed* unit of the Hungarian Second Army that was fighting with the Germans against the Soviets. Conscripts like Wald's father and uncle were not allowed to bear arms because Jews were considered "unworthy." Given the rampant anti-Semitism in the Hungarian military, being engaged in forced labor on the Eastern Front became lethal for Jews. If conscripts did not die from assignments like having to bury the dead on the forward lines without any kind of protection while bullets from both sides of the struggle flew past, they easily fell prey to being murdered outright by Hungarian soldiers.[30]

When George Wald was conscripted, Ibolya was pregnant with Wald's brother John. She was left to raise the children on her own. Her desperation about saving her family escalated when the Nazi occupation began in March 1944. Shortly afterward, all Jews were obligated to wear the yellow star.[31] Ibolya was intent on finding a way, any way, to protect her children from impending harm.

The period from Wald's father's conscription into forced labor until the end of the war, when Wald turned eight years old, was for the young girl a time of irrational chaos and terror. Targeted for being Jews, her once-assimilated family that had lived comfortably among liberal, observing Catholics at 48 Pozsonyi Ut was now broken up, forced to wear markers, and under constant threat of annihilation.[32]

To a child, the dire situation, inexplicable by logic, must have unfolded like a nightmare. Thus, the family's uncanny ability to survive must have seemed miraculous.

Ibolya, with her non-Jewish good looks, risked not wearing a yellow star and circulated during the day to discover ways to save her family. Eventually, she met a Catholic priest she trusted who convinced her to convert to Catholicism along with her children to save their lives.

Ibolya knew that the Second Jewish Law of 1939 prevented Jews from using conversion to Catholicism as a way to hide their "racial" identity and would ultimately not save them from deportation. Nevertheless, knowing full well that her true identity could be "uncovered," Ibolya converted to Catholicism in May 1944. She anguished over not having other options and felt totally unclear about the consequences, especially for her children, but she didn't know what else to do. She hoped the "cover" of Catholicism could at the very least extend her children's lives if not her own. The well-meaning priest later died himself while defending a girls' orphanage.[33]

Wald suspects that her mother—who all along was seeking ways to release Wald's father and uncle from forced labor—must have heard about Raoul Wallenberg's arrival in Budapest in July 1944. Wallenberg, from a prominent Christian family, was the Swedish businessman commissioned by the United States War Refugee Board and the Swedish Legation in Hungary to save the Jews of Budapest from deportation.[34] Wallenberg had worked for a Dutch bank in Haifa in 1935 and met Jews there who had escaped Hitler's Germany. Learning of their persecutions by the Nazis affected him deeply. Wallenberg's own great, great grandfather Benedicks was Jewish. Dr. Karl Lauer, a Hungarian Jew who was co-owner with Wallenberg of an international trading company, and whose movement through Europe was restricted when Nazis rose to power, recommended Wallenberg to represent the Swedish Legation in Hungary.[35]

By the time Wallenberg arrived in Budapest, nearly 440,000 Hungarian Jews had already been deported from the countryside mainly to Auschwitz-Birkenau. Then in October 1944, the Hungarian Arrow Cross Party collaborated with the SS under Eichmann's command to mount a reign of terror against the Budapest Jews. German authorities murdered eighty thousand Jews, while tens of thousands of others were forced west to the Hungarian-Austrian border on death marches.[36]

During that autumn, Wallenberg used War Refugee Board and Swedish funds to establish hospitals, nurseries, and soup kitchens, and to designate more than thirty "safe" houses that together formed the core of what was called the international "ghetto" in Budapest. This so-called "ghetto," which saved Jews from deportation, was reserved for Jewish families holding certificates of protection from neutral countries, such as Sweden. Wallenberg distributed thousands of certificates of protection to Jews and secured their release both with the certificates and with other forged documents.[37] Wald believes her mother had direct contact with Wallenberg. In a personal letter to me, Wald wrote:

> I have a copy of a document from Wallenberg from November 1945 stating that our family was under Swedish protection, free from the obligation to use the yellow star, to live in buildings marked with it or to serve in the forced labor camps. I believe this document helped my mother to get my father and my uncle out of the camp.[38]

In November 1945, George Wald returned home from forced labor, fortunate not to have been among the 80 percent of Jews who did *not* return, many of them having been slaughtered by the Hungarian military.[39] George and his brother-in-law returned emaciated from having laid railroad tracks amidst constant bombing by the US Air Force in Györ, on the Danube, midway between Vienna and Budapest. George had dwindled down to half his size, from the hefty 105 kilos he weighed when he had left to a meager 48 kilos. Wald remembers feeling at age eight that she was stronger than her father.[40]

George was terribly grieved to find that all three members of his family had converted to Catholicism. However, perhaps sadly realizing that the cover might help them survive, he himself "became" Lutheran. When the Walds were finally forced to abandon their apartment on Pozsonyi Ut, Wallenberg helped them relocate to a tiny room in one of the large, seven- or eight-story-high "safe houses." But by December, during the Soviet siege of Budapest, all Jews in the safe house the Walds occupied were commanded to evacuate to be taken to Auschwitz.[41]

On the designated day, people were told to carry only what they could wear on their bodies. Wald's father warned her mother not to hurry, saying they would have to be the last ones to leave the building. He seemed to be familiar with a plan Wallenberg had organized.

Wald remembers that they were at the very end of the long line waiting in the snow before the marching began. As was customary, a buggy had come loaded with food supplies for the whole building. But this time the food was not being distributed. Wallenberg seemed to appear out of nowhere. He instructed Wald's family to stay immediately behind the buggy, to move along with it as it pressed forward around a street corner, and to not look back. Wallenberg personally pulled Wald's family out of the lineup as the marchers, now moving forward, slowly receded from their view. He led the family to the Swedish Legacy. Once there, directly in view of the war zone, Wald experienced some incredible incidents.

She was to be sleeping in a room in the Legacy in an armchair near a window. She could hear and see the bombs Americans were dropping from the air, while Ukrainians of the Soviet Army were fighting on the streets. She heard a horribly vast explosion as the Americans hit a high school nearby that was being used as a weapons warehouse. It seemed to her as if every window in the city broke, including the one by her chair, which was smashed to smithereens. Shrapnel from the bomb exploded into her room. To her great shock, she was the only one in the room whose skin had not been penetrated by the glass shards flying above her head.

As bombs continued to burst, and the room became more crowded, Wald remembers being ushered to the basement. But her mother, determined that her children not be infected with lice, scooped up the two children to reach a spot where they could be bathed. Wald remembered seeing armed Soviet troops advancing from door to door, fighting to take Budapest from the Germans, as the Germans shot back from the other side of the boulevard.[42]

Wartime for the Walds was a contagion of "fear" and "fog," Wald wrote in *Windows*. The muffled adult conversations she heard about war stirred her worries: "They . . . take me to a side of the room. I cannot know what is going on. I just experience the anxiety and the constant fear. It is a fear I have too, not of them, but of something they themselves fear." She continued, "The bomb didn't fall on our building but on the one next to ours," and the neighbors were "buried in the rubble." The rubble, she recalled her mother saying, "could become their *tomb*," a chilling word Wald was hearing for the first time.[43] Once again, Wald survived, a witness to violence and death surrounding her.

During our interviews, Wald often told me she owed her life to Raoul Wallenberg. A non-Jewish rescuer like Oskar Schindler, Wallenberg saved Jews on an even larger scale. He identified passionately with the plight of innocent Jewish victims and was driven to save one hundred thousand of them. Ironically, after the war, Wallenberg's rescue work may have caused him to lose his life. Shortly after the Soviets took the city, they detained him somewhere outside of Budapest for reasons never definitively known, and he subsequently disappeared.[44]

Since childhood, Wald has had to ponder dramatic paradoxes. Fear filled her earliest years because, as a Jew, she was the target of irrational Nazi prejudice and hate. At the same time, her rescue was due to the extraordinary generosity and courage of non-Jews. These contradictions challenged her at a young age to process and try to make sense of human moral complexities.

The Cover of Catholicism: Creating a Double Identity

After Wallenberg rescued Wald's family, the Soviet Army took the city of Budapest. New coalition governments formed that included several existing political parties: Independent Smallholders, Social Democrats, and Hungarian Communists, among others. Mátyás Rákosi, Stalin's puppet in Hungary, introduced a gradualist approach toward turning Hungary's government into a Soviet-style political, economic, and social system. The Allies still had troops in Europe in 1945, and Stalin wished to deflect Western criticism of rapid Communist takeovers. Nevertheless, the coalition government immediately redistributed land which it took from large estate owners and gave to peasants. Wald remembers people feeling the influence of Rákosi's declaration: "Those who don't work with their hands don't eat." Communists took full control of the country in 1949.[45]

Wald's family experienced famine immediately after the war. The Walds were still sharing a small apartment in a building with another family, waiting for their own apartment on Pozsonyi Ut to be rebuilt after it had been bombed during the siege of the city. The eight-year-old Wald recalled her neighbors gathering with knives in the snow around a "skin-to-bone-lean horse" that had died, "probably from hunger," and their taking "whatever flesh" was "left on it."[46] Wald's mother did not participate in the butchery.

Wald had recently converted to Catholicism and felt desperate to shed insecurities she was trying hard not to internalize. She found solace and refuge in a quiet yard where, with her agile body, she performed self-styled gymnastics on a high bar.

> I play in the yard of another building where we stay since we left the Swedish Legacy. . . . There is a contraption made from two upright pieces of lumber that hold a cross bar meant to put carpets on. . . . I can . . . raise myself to it, put my hip on the bar and swing around head down and up again. I love doing this.[47]

After making her First Communion, Wald invested that yard with deep layers of spiritual meaning whenever she escaped there to be alone. But in *Windows*, her heightened experience is not actually narrated by the first-person "I" voice of previous sections. Rather, a new voice spontaneously enters the narrative, a character named Agnes—a duplicate of Susana, a second self—who describes Susana's Communion as if it were her own and the yard as if it had become her private, mystical, and magical place:

> Agnes . . . tells me: "I have taken First Communion. I feel a great inner glow . . . I talk with the presence that is in me now. I see everything in a different light. The yard where I play on the crossbar is now the place I go to be alone. I have this moment of total intimacy, alone in the yard. . . . I want to visit it often, live and stay in it. I learn to do this everywhere. I can be inside me even when I am with others. I can take this insideness with me wherever I go."[48]

Susana seems to have created Agnes, her double, as a way of coping with the conversion to Catholicism. Agnes transports Susana to a place of sanctuary apart from frightening religious, social, and political upheavals. Agnes has the ability to "discover . . . the psychological . . . more spiritual aspects of reality" that rise above adult "fear" and "fog" and that help her counterpart Susana to transcend the rupture from Jewish to Catholic that conversion has imposed upon her.[49]

Agnes' descriptions of Catholic iconography reveal Wald's search for integration between her Jewish core identity and her Catholic "cover" so that the inner, spiritual life she is trying to nurture and preserve may be sustained with some degree of continuity.

Agnes finds an embedded suffering in both Christian and Jewish traditions that allows Wald to believe she is still Jewish, though converted. Agnes helps Wald see Jesus in terms reminiscent of the experience of persecuted Hungarian Jews. Agnes tells Wald that she weeps when she sees "an image of the Man of Sorrows" in an Orthodox church. The image makes Agnes think of "the aria in Handel's *Messiah* when the contralto sings, 'He was despised and neglected and acquainted with grief.'" It was the first time, Agnes says, that she realized an image "can change you, move you, make you *feel*."[50]

Agnes recounts that, for her, the Saturday night and Sunday morning of Holy Week are deeply moving, with the consecration of the new fire and the new water and living through Jesus' death and resurrection. But all the while that Agnes/Wald is filled with awe and wonder by Catholic ritual, she's thinking of Jesus as a Jew. And when the priest advises her during confession not ever to say she's Jewish, she knows he's trying to protect her as a Jew.[51]

Wald's conversion to Catholicism began her lifelong need to wear different outer/public layers of identity to protect her original Jewish core. In each successive environment she lived—Hungary, Argentina, Chile, Canada, and Mexico—she experienced her Jewish core as being under siege, though to differing degrees. However severe her fears became, whether more or less, hiding Jewishness became a condition of her being. As her cover identity shifted and changed, her motivation remained consistent: to seek refuge from being targeted and possibly annihilated as a Jew. In *Windows,* she writes metaphorically about layers of identity: "That there can be many eyes on one face, one façade, seems only natural to me."[52] A face is a façade. The essence of a person that lives and breathes behind masks of "many eyes" is something much deeper.

When World War II ended, Wald was in the ironic position of needing to hide her newly found Catholic cover. It was dangerous to be a practicing Catholic in Soviet-controlled Hungary, but the young Wald did not fully understand the situation. She knew that outside the church there was no talk of God. She knew that her mother, still a convert to Catholicism, did not attend church even once. But the young Wald did not understand political realities.[53]

Conversion to Catholicism had been different for Susana than it had been for her mother. For Ibolya, becoming Catholic under Nazi rule was simply a survival strategy. But Ibolya knew that living as a Catholic under the Soviets would not protect her from Communist anti-religious politics. She became a Catholic in name only. For the young Susana, on the other hand, becoming Catholic—even in her own way—had been a method to resolve her crisis of identity, a way for her to access the spirituality she needed for her well-being and self-nurturance, regardless of the political forces surrounding her. Initially, she didn't realize that as a practicing Catholic under the Soviets, she was once again vulnerable. However, even when she became aware of the political dangers, she remained dependent on religious observance, given her spiritual needs.

The Hungarian Catholic Church in the emerging Communist nation was led by Cardinal József Mindszenty, Archbishop of Esztergom, who had been an outspoken opponent of Nazism. Seeing his people come under increasingly tight Soviet influence beginning in 1947, the cardinal urged Hungarians not to give up their schools or their land to the Communists, who wanted all Catholic schools nationalized. In December 1948, the cardinal wrote an open pastoral letter calling Communism "an atheistic theology" opposed to "the spirit of the Church."[54]

By Christmas of that year, when the cardinal's letter became public, he was arrested, since the state viewed him as "the center of counter revolutionary forces." The arrest was the government's attempt to remove the last great political figure to resist the state's spread of monolithic power.[55]

During our interviews, Wald never mentioned the conflict between the Communist state in Hungary and the cardinal's leadership. She was, of course, just a girl of nine or ten at the time. But she did perceive how her lessons in school had changed under the newly formed coalition government, shortly after the Soviets rid Hungary of Nazis. Under the new Hungarian Republic, her classes emphasized nationalism and the political unification movements across Europe in 1848, including the unification of Hungary. Very subtly, religion was being subordinated to the state, as when the old national anthem was abandoned because it requested that the Lord bless the Hungarians: *Isten ald meg a magyart.*[56]

By 1949 the Communists gained complete control of Hungary. They reframed a constitution that was a carbon copy of the Soviet constitution, and the country became the People's Republic of Hungary.[57] But the young Wald was still underestimating the degree to which one's Catholicism needed to be underplayed and hidden.

Apparently sensing that their daughter's avid churchgoing could be dangerous in such a secular, authoritarian political context, Wald's parents forbade her to attend church. The thought of being separated once again from her spiritual refuge must have felt devastating to Wald.

The ten-year-old Wald rebelled by fleeing from home and defying her parents' order. Ibolya and George were distraught, not knowing where their daughter had fled.[58] Wald may have viewed the church as a more formal version of the simple yard where she first experienced sanctuary. She may not have understood, as her parents did, the possible political consequences of being visibly devoted to Catholicism.

Eventually, the Walds found their daughter. Finally understanding the importance of spirituality to Susana's emotional well-being, they relented by allowing her once again to attend church services, though they were reluctant and apprehensive.

As a very young Jew, Wald had seen her burgeoning inner world threatened with decimation under Nazism. Now as a Jewish preteen in Stalinist-controlled Hungary using the cover of Catholicism to express her transcendent yearnings, Wald saw that both her spiritual/cultural core and her cover religion were running counter to political realities on the ground and her parents' protective pragmatism.

Reconnecting with a Jewish Past

With the help of his well-to-do older brother who lived in Argentina, Wald's father arranged for his family to escape from Stalinist Hungary in 1949 and to relocate in Buenos Aires, a Spanish-speaking melting pot that was dominantly Christian. Wald remembered no specifically Jewish neighborhood in the city, but her extended family met regularly every month in the company of a network of mainly Jewish friends. Their gatherings took place in her uncle's home, the one who helped them to resettle in that city.[59]

This informal community of Jews was actively engaged in intellectual discussion about the arts, classical music, and film. Wald and her mother bonded by going to the cinema each week and discussing the films with each other.

Wald remembers being asked by her schoolmates in Buenos Aires when she was thirteen, "Are you Russian?" She did not realize the question was a code for asking, "Are you Jewish?" The majority of Jews in the city at that time had emigrated from pogroms in Russia earlier in the century. Innocently, she answered, "No, I'm Hungarian."[60] Even if she *had* understood her schoolmates' subtle allusion to Jewish religious identity, Wald was not ready to expose herself as Jewish. She was still observing Catholicism, even while her family was attempting to assimilate as cultural Jews into Buenos Aires' society.

In the neighborhood where Wald lived at 3791 Nueva York Street, she had for the first time a room of her own, a space in which she loved to hide, all alone. Her mother paid attention to Wald's emerging womanhood and created the space as feminine, with a pink carpet. Her mother's piano was also in the room, where both she and Wald played their music. Wald remembered the small, modern Bakelite radio that sat on the piano. She enjoyed listening especially to the program about the lives of the exemplary Saints of the Day and their heroic martyrdoms, introduced by Massenet's *Meditation de Thais.*

Now it was the pink-carpeted room that became Wald's sanctuary, much in the way the yard in Budapest and the Catholic Church had been her places of refuge. We know from Wald's late-life memoir, *Windows,* that years later, just the memory of that room could bring her comfort and strength. In one segment of *Windows,* Wald reminisces with her inner self, Agnes, about the time she was sixty-two and feeling unsettled by great personal transformation. She remembers gaining strength and comfort by reflecting back on her childhood experience of her room, when she felt possessed by a female energy:

> I tell Agnes: ". . . At this time in life this room feels to be as vast as the universe, filled with a presence that is alive, dark, with no specific shape, name or identity. It is inconceivably big, fuller than full, filling. It is immeasurable energy, strength and female essence."[61]

At another point in the memoir, Wald tells Agnes that she remembers listening with her eyes closed to her mother playing her piano and hearing

"how the music rises, expands, further, faster, lighter toward the sun."
Agnes responds by saying she can also hear Wald's mother:

> ... The way she would be submerged in her music, away from us,
> from it all, for a moment free, flying high, then coming back. I
> believe it is this same impulse towards the Absolute that moved
> Ibolya and myself towards a groping for religion, a way of tran-
> scending through prayer and meditation.

Wald answers Agnes by saying that "this kind of feeling as our mother
was moving into another reality, another space, another free vastness" is
"what has made me an artist."[62]

These dialogues with Agnes in Wald's memoir illuminate the connections Wald's reflective mind forged between her early desires for
transcendence and freedom and her later need to create art. Wald's
imagination and spirit yearned to soar freely, to reach beyond material
boundaries and the self to touch "another reality," a "presence" that was
"vast as the universe," a "free vastness."

Wald/Agnes imagines that the pathways to this otherworldly dimension can be both religious and aesthetic, pathways imitating the combined
religious and aesthetic leanings Wald observed in her own mother. Wald/
Agnes may have been thinking of Ibolya's ritual lighting of memorial
candles for deceased family members, her love of Bartók's music, and her
meditative fasts during the Days of Awe.

Though Wald's childhood in Budapest had thwarted her from developing a consistent religious practice, in Buenos Aires her extended family
life and active social network introduced her as a teen to freedoms she
could experience as an assimilated cultural Jew. With family and friends,
she frequented concerts of the Philharmonic Opera, engaged in discussions of wide-ranging topics from Sartre to Communism, and pondered
the different careers she might pursue.[63]

Wald became a student at the Escuela Nacional de Cerámica in
Buenos Aires where she learned the technical and artistic aspects of
ceramics, specializing in the treatment of ceramic surfaces. This training
provided her with a foundation for her later work creating murals for
public buildings. But had she not expanded her vision of art beyond the
technical, she told me she would have wound up as a mainly decorative

artist and not the Surrealist she later became. She had wanted to enter university, but such education had been reserved by her family for her brother. It was an exclusion she eventually hoped to overcome.[64]

At age seventeen in 1955, her fourth year at Escuela Nacional de Cerámica, Wald met José Hausner at the home wedding celebration of two of her Jewish friends. Hausner was, like her, a Holocaust survivor, but his experience had been more devastating. His family was from one of the Hungarian peripheries where the country's deportations of Jews to Auschwitz had begun. He was the only member of his immediate family to survive the death camp and found it almost impossible to talk about the terrors he experienced there. He had been deported with his brother and stepmother after being arrested on the same day that he turned eighteen and received his high school degree. His father, who was the owner of a small shoe factory, was deported the previous day. Hausner survived only because Josef Mengele "selected" him for his exceptional physical ability. He was saved from death because he was a bronze medal gymnast.[65]

The Holocaust past that Wald shared with Hausner bound them tightly. Both were intent on repressing their fears and horrific memories. Hausner was living as an assimilated Jew, attempting to blend into the melting pot. Wald had a loving courtship with him for two years. They married the same year that Wald graduated from Escuela Nacional de Cerámica.[66]

Wald realized much before she married Hausner that she had to end her relationship with the Catholic Church. When the Church required her to believe a newly issued dogma, her past experience of Catholicism as liberating was contradicted. Church dogma came to feel more like an obstruction to personal freedom than a route to spiritual transcendence. Wald told her confessor in Buenos Aires that she could not accept the Church's view of faith as obligation.[67]

Being in sympathetic partnership with Hausner, whose past losses and suffering were so palpable they were too painful for him to revisit, Wald may have felt even more acutely than before the need to preserve the Jewish core she was suppressing. To accept the Catholic Church's dogma may have felt like an erasure, and thus an utter violation, of her own and her husband's personal histories. Moreover, her search for transcendence and spiritual connection, for the "free vastness" beyond material reality that she needed for artistic inspiration, would have been impeded by dogma that required strict adherence. In launching her career as a ceramic artist, she held freedom from any sort of dogma as a primary element of her self-definition.

Seven years after Wald and Hausner moved to Chile, when Wald became immersed in the Surrealist path, she found other language to articulate what had been her automatic resistance to the Church's requirement. The Surrealists she met and studied in the late 1960s opposed the repression of personal freedom required by all politically organized structures. They considered organized religions to be political structures just as totalitarian governments were.[68]

The Hausners moved to Santiago, Chile, in 1957 after José completed the commission for which he had been sent to Buenos Aires by his employer, National Cash Register— to write a book on the mechanization of banking. Once in Santiago, José and Susana had two children whom they raised without Jewish religious observance. Nevertheless, the children were deeply conscious of their parents' Holocaust past and knew they were Jewish. One could consider the family's Jewish identification covert, since Hausner shared publicly the details of his experiences at Auschwitz-Birkenau only much later in his life. Their son was not circumcised, and their basic attitude going forward was that, for the sake of their own humanity, they must simply carry on as nonpracticing Jews.[69]

Wald set up an art studio in Santiago, hopeful that her work in ceramics would receive attention. In Buenos Aires as an art student, her work had been shown every year in an important gallery with the work of her student colleagues. It was only one year after she graduated that she and Hausner left for Chile.

Another New and Dangerous Sanctuary in Surrealism

During Wald's first four years in Santiago, she continued creating ceramic pieces and murals. She became open to other horizons as well and began pursuing an entirely different path. In 1962 she began studying brain physiology in the School of Medicine at the University of Santiago. During this same period, she worked for a salary in the genetics lab.[70]

While she was engaged at the university doing investigative medical research, she met Ludwig Zeller, the curator for the Ministry of Education Art Gallery. Zeller was a poet and scholar responsible for three art galleries in Santiago. He was also employed in the medical school. As part of the faculty of the Medical Anthropology department, he was an expert in verbal communication studying, among other things, "the disintegration of language in the mentally ill."[71]

Wald and Zeller met on a cold, rainy morning in May 1963 at a campus art opening that Zeller himself had curated, held in the Students' Center of the School of Medicine. Their chance meeting changed the course of Wald's life. Immensely productive, their relationship opened Wald to the world of Surrealism and its own particular way of fusing art, politics, and spirituality.

Zeller was from a German Christian background—his father Bavarian, his mother from an established Chilean family. Though neither of his parents were practicing Catholics, Zeller was a seeker of the absolute who had entered the Jesuit order but left it after four years. With his wife, who was Jewish, he studied, translated, and published several German Romantic writers in whom he found the roots of Surrealism. However, the thrust of his involvement in Surrealism derived from his passionate interest in the Post World War I climate of literary experimentation originally created in Chile by Vicente Huidobro (1893–1948) and in Argentina by Aldo Pellegrini (1903–1973).[72]

Huidobro, who traveled frequently to France and Madrid, brought a reverence for poetics to Chilean writing that Zeller absorbed. Huidobro supported the formation of the first Chilean Surrealist group Mandrágora (the Mandrake) in 1938. Zeller read their poetry and articles voraciously, and later with Wald formed the second generation of Chilean Surrealists.[73]

Wald and Zeller's literary and aesthetic philosophy was influenced also by South America's first Surrealist group, formed by the poet Pellegrini in Argentina in 1926. Pellegrini was deeply affected by the *Surrealist Manifesto* of 1924 written by Surrealism's founder André Breton. According to Pellegrini, this vanguard movement called for total freedom in the arts, arts devoted to the imagination and divorced from reason, from literary, aesthetic, and social norms, and from all prohibitions, prejudice, and fear. These formative Surrealist ideas spread to Venezuela and Peru as well.[74]

The Surrealism that Zeller introduced to Wald nourished not only her relationship to him, but also her thinking and artwork throughout the next six decades. Surrealism appealed to her desire to link the "free vastness" to which she aspired with artistic creation and offered her the possibility of once again unleashing her own creative sparks. The Surrealist idea that unlocking the unconscious could lead to healing, creative expression, and the transformation of consciousness reinvigorated Wald the artist. Moreover, Surrealism also forecasted the potential of artistic expression to change social conditions.

Rather than merely an artistic and literary style, Surrealism is a revolutionary approach to life that stresses the need for nonconformity and the primacy of dreams and the unconscious over the limitations of reason. Since the dominance of Enlightenment "reason" in the West had culminated in the absurdity of world war at the outset of the twentieth century and the rise of fascism, founder André Breton posited Surrealism to be the antidote—the liberation of "our actual functioning of thought" without the misguided "control exercised by reason."[75]

Also in the 1920s, Breton's Jewish colleagues—Tristan Tzara in Romania (a colleague of Huidobro) and the Janco brothers, Marcel and Georges, in Hungary—founded the Dada movement, which was devoted to using art to counter European cultural conventions and institutional frameworks. Tzara, born Samuel Rosenstock, and the Janco brothers, had, like Wald, been subjected to pervasive anti-Semitism. Along with the Surrealists, their collective voices articulated a revolt against war and fascism. Further, they brought a Jewish insistence on justice to the repair of the world, *tikkun olam*.[76]

At the May 1963 art opening where Wald met Zeller, Zeller's immediate interest in Wald's art inspired her. She told him of her diploma in ceramics. He wished to see her studio. Impressed, he offered her a show, and Wald got her ceramics studio going again. The show was inaugurated in November. All her ceramic pieces sold out.[77]

Wald and Zeller became close friends who collaborated artistically and intellectually. Wald took breaks from her lab work and used space Zeller provided at his office. There she worked in ink on French papers while music played. Zeller shared his poetry with her. By 1968, they produced their first collaborative volume, *The Rules of the Game*, poetry by Zeller that Wald illustrated, published by Ediciones Casa de la Luna, the publishing company they founded together.[78]

All along, Surrealism guided them. Surrealism was now the cover that most aptly provided Wald's spiritual nature and artistic tendencies with sanctuary. Zeller's attraction to Surrealism was matched by Wald's, and their attraction to one another then became all-consuming. It was extremely difficult for them to come together as a couple, though, since both were already married with children. Wald and Hausner underwent therapy for a year to save their marriage, but Wald ultimately decided to move out on her own with her children. Zeller moved in with her in 1966.[79]

For Wald, the relationship with Zeller and Surrealism offered outlets and possibilities on many levels: mystical, psychological, artistic, and political. Surrealism also extended the concept of freedom to the area of eroticism, which was viewed, according to art critic Alyce Mahon, as a "primary means of unsettling and interrogating reality." The Surrealists used Eros as a "political device" for expressing "social commentary in their art, their writing and in their interactive exhibition spaces."[80]

From 1963 until 1970, the artistic and literary collaborations of Wald and Zeller marked them as activists engaged in critiquing the restraining conventions of Chilean society and culture. Zeller was well-positioned for a year or two to secure support for their projects in his status as curator of the Ministry of Education. Then, when Zeller had to leave his post, they worked as freelancers in graphic design. Zeller took on other curatorial jobs; Wald taught ceramics. Together their publishing venture, Ediciones Casa de la Luna, produced books and a magazine. Casa de la Luna was also a cultural center in downtown Santiago that exhibited contemporary art and sponsored conferences, experimental film screenings, and "happenings."[81]

Many of these events turned the political tide against them. They realized their endangered position when Salvador Allende, a Socialist in alliance with Communists, won the violently contested race for president of Chile in October 1970. The two main issues were the nationalization of the country's copper mines (then owned by United States corporations) and more equitable distribution of wealth throughout the country, issues creating violent divisions between the classes.[82]

Allende's reliance on Communist support to win the election created disturbance for the new regime, the first leftist administration ever voted in by a democratic nation. The regime needed primarily to demonstrate its ability to stave off the rumored, right-wing military coup d'etat waiting in the wings. The atmosphere of urgency and danger escalated when two days before Allende was confirmed by Congress, the commander in chief of the Chilean military, on whom Allende depended to uphold the nation's constitution and democratic processes, was murdered by an insider during an attempted kidnapping supported by the CIA.[83]

It was just three months before the murder of the commander in chief and Allende's precarious victory, that Zeller and Wald's "happening," *Surrealism in Chile,* drew huge crowds and was shown live on the Catholic University's popular TV station. The pièce de résistance was Zeller and Wald's hanging mannequin, *Presidenciable,* the effigy of a presidential candidate, intended perhaps as a prescient and ironic vision of the fate awaiting whomever would become the political victor. Wald told me in an interview that she, Zeller, and all the artists in their circle knew a coup d'etat was inevitable.[84]

Wald's main contribution to the "happening," she wrote in her memoir, was an extraordinary floor painting made in collaboration with two other painters that obliged "the public to participate in the surreality of the event." Wald required all visitors to the exhibit to remove their shoes before entering, a custom "unheard of in Chilean society." A large poster at the entrance read, "Jesus walked barefoot, most of the world's population has no shoes, take off yours." When a nun remarked that her vows didn't allow her to take her shoes off, Wald responded that "unfortunately you won't be able to see the show."[85]

Wald completed the painting just twelve hours before the show opened, feverishly working with artists Valentina Cruz and Viterbo Sepúlveda. She described their process in her memoir:

> Viterbo traces the testicles that . . . correspond to the phallus-shaped paper cutout made by Ludwig stuck to the wall. I find it especially satisfying to trace the outlines of very large-scale body parts with movements of my whole being, not just my hands or

arms. . . . Ludwig . . . glues to the floor some fake breasts he bought; one becomes a clitoris over a gigantic female sex; another two are nipples of large breast. . . . At six in the morning we are done.[86]

The exhibit also included Nemesio Antunúz's grotesquely comic, life-sized, soft sculpture dolls mechanically scratching their bellies with long, translucent nails; rubber foam body parts by Valentina Cruz displayed in jars of water as if they were pickled; and artifacts from Santiago's main prison that illustrated the fantasies of inmates with erotic allusions.[87]

It is perhaps not surprising that Wald and Zeller's "happenings" caused them to be viewed by Allende's Communist-allied administration as "shit disturbers." First, four different posts that they held were given over to Communist Party members. Then they were advised to leave the country by Communist Party members they knew who had read their names in various Communist articles. The left-wing radicalization of Allende's government confirmed in the couple's minds that a right-wing coup was inevitable, and they knew that under a right-wing coup, their vulnerability would be even more certain. After they left Chile, they heard that on the first day of the coup, people were killed in front of their cultural center.[88]

Undoubtedly, the childhood fears Wald felt under Stalinist Communism in Hungary must have been revived in her mind. She and Zeller were without their jobs, had no money, and felt trapped, without choices. They decided to leave the country for Toronto, Canada, where Wald had a long-standing friend who had emigrated earlier. Wald left Santiago in December, and in January Zeller followed with their baby son, leaving behind their home, their books, and their studios.[89] The upheaval brought them face-to-face with the devastating consequences of living as Surrealists under a rigid regime, whether left- or right-wing.

A Surrealist in Spite of Surrealism: Transcendence and Gender

Wald and Zeller chose to reside in Toronto where the artist and muralist Carmen Cereceda had already moved.[90] Wald's life in Toronto was active and full—teaching art at Sheridan College, developing further her literary and artistic relationship with Zeller, collaborating with him on Surrealist projects, and eventually shifting her own approach to Surrealism in feminist directions, countering resistance she faced in the 1970s from members of *Phases*, a Surrealist group centered in Paris with which she and Zeller affiliated. She was one of several women Surrealists—like her seniors, the painters Leonora Carrington, Remedios Varo, and Dorothea Tanning, and the photographers Lee Miller, Dora Maar, and Kati Horna—to become empowered by feminism's cross-cultural reach and extend the philosophy of Surrealism to the expression of women's themes in their lives and art.[91]

Wald's Jewish identity once again hovered below the surface, not overtly visible. She did not, for example, identify with the Russian Jews in Toronto who tended to remain within their own communities without integrating themselves into mainstream culture. But her children were thoroughly aware of their mother's deep identification as Jewish and as adults were attracted to Jewish partners.[92]

Wald's muted Jewish identity needed an outlet for its impulse toward a spiritual aesthetics that would circumvent the confines of traditional, religious ritual and polarizing, political movements. She found direction from the feminist spirituality movement that was creating universalist female images of wisdom and power.[93]

She began integrating a decidedly spiritual dimension into her practice of Surrealism, a dimension significantly influenced by her reading of Jungian feminists who explored ancient archetypes and myths that included several mystical and feminine aspects of Judaism. In so doing, she was moving in different directions than Surrealists who were in lockstep with political directions Surrealism had taken.[94]

From the outset, Wald's Surrealism had involved her belief in a transcendent reality above and beyond everyday experience. That transcendent realm could be reached by meshing spiritual yearning with aesthetic expression in different forms of art. In the 1970s, when she and Zeller were becoming acclimated to Toronto, they maintained their affiliation with Surrealists internationally who still debated the two different directions in which Breton, who had died in 1966, navigated the movement. Breton held Surrealism to both Marxist political and psychological/ spiritual standards, but the tensions between the two never harmoniously reconciled and caused divisions within the movement.[95]

The first breach Wald experienced with Surrealism appeared in her rejection of the political dogma associated with Marxism and with

Breton's seeming intoxication with Leon Trotsky and Communism.[96] While Breton fluctuated in his inclusion of political ideology in Surrealism, an example being his co-authorship of "For a Revolutionary Independent Art" in 1938 with Trotsky, Wald never departed from the original tenets of 1924 where Breton links artistic freedom to an *attitude* of revolt rather than a politics of revolt. According to Wald, it will be culture, not politics, that will save humanity.[97]

With Breton in his 1924 *Manifesto*, Wald sees the artist in revolt against the fetters of rationalism, habit, and imposed structures of thought. To this end, perception, and not politics, need to be rejuvenated so that the activity of the mind will be inspired by imagination and desire to reach for the realization of human potential. These are ideas with which Wald continues to sympathize. For her, the Surrealist artist values the spirit of revolt more highly than politics. Wald told me she had deep doubts about politics, and that it is "within culture" that "each of us separately can reach deep, psychological levels." Only then can "we have the chance to come together." It was because Wald connected Surrealism with the spirit of revolt, and not the politics of it, that she was able to sustain Surrealism as one of the covers over her transcendent yearnings.[98]

I suspect that had Wald not been able also to include her identity as a woman under the umbrella of Surrealism, she would have had to abandon the shelter Surrealism provided over her spiritual nature. Though she had to create a separation between herself and more mainstream Surrealists, she was nevertheless able to incorporate her type of feminism into her perspective as a Surrealist artist and writer. In this, she was not unlike many women associated with the Surrealist movement who, according to art historian Patricia Allmer, subsequently subverted gender categories and the traditions of art to show that tradition is not a fixed entity and that out of tradition new forms would be produced.[99]

Wald's feminist transformation, which began in the 1970s with the advent of such publications as *Ms.* magazine, deepened as she read psychological works on the concept of the feminine by Carl Jung and Erich Neumann. In Neumann's *The Great Mother*, the feminine archetype emerges from a Jungian collective unconscious shared by all of humanity and manifests itself cross-culturally and over time with attributes that can be described as fascinating, terrible, overpowering, and eventually divine.

The archetype specifically associated with "Sofia" evolved through human history, first as an embodiment of wisdom and ultimately as manifestation of spirit and divinity. In this context, Wald could trace the emergence of the feminine face of God that appears in mystical Jewish tradition, the Shekinah, the presence of God that dwells among the people. In Wald's letter to me of November 15, 2018, she wrote:

> My exploration of the feminine goes parallel with mystical ideas such as the concept of Shekinah or the *Great Mother* archetype in the analysis of Erich Neumann. In the vision of the latter there appears a many thousand years' process of spiritualization of the feminine archetype. His analysis rings true to me, and it is the basis of the thinking of feminist analysts like Jean Shinoda Bolen or Betty De Shong Meador.[100]

Wald became so moved by the work of Jungian feminist Betty De Shong Meador that she translated into Spanish Meador's book *Inanna, Lady of the Largest Heart.* This book, appearing in 2009, presents to readers Enheduanna, the Sumerian poet who lived around 2,300 BCE. Wald felt compelled to bring Enheduanna's story to a Mexican audience.[101] By that time, she and Zeller had been living in Oaxaca for fifteen years.

Enheduanna was a governor of Ur and a high priestess to the moon god Nanna. Her poems in praise of Nanna's daughter, the goddess Inanna, are the first literary works of a known historical author. Wald's foray into ancient spirituality through Meador's work brought her close to issues in the Hebrew Bible, since the patriarch Abraham, the first Hebrew, also lived in Ur, though five hundred years later than Enheduanna. Enheduanna's poems to the goddess Inanna characterize the goddess as "the active feminine principle in nature"—lusty, full of raw energy, powerful. In the Hebrew Bible, Inanna, the Sumerian goddess, frequently appears carrying an Akkadian name, Ishtar. It is probable that Enheduanna's poems to Inanna/Ishtar, which were popular for fifteen hundred years, were part of the Sumerian/Akkadian culture Abraham inherited and was then destined to leave.[102]

At the same time Wald's thinking was becoming influenced by feminist ideas, she and Zeller were active in the second tier of Surrealists, the *Phases* artistic and literary movement centered in Paris that Breton

Enheduanna's Message

continued to foster until his death. Beginning in 1974 and "for eleven consecutive years," Wald wrote in her memoir, "we visit Paris, and . . . letters, books, all kinds of documents come and go" between she and Zeller and Édouard Jaguer, the movement's founder.[103]

Jaguer presented Zeller's collages and poetry and Wald's drawings in his "very successful, beautiful magazine called, of course, *Phases*," and "it is through his publications, his introductions" that Wald and Zeller "meet painters like Eugenio Granell, Mayo, Guy Roussile, Philip West" and become their "collaborators." Their communication with Granell, an exile of the Spanish Civil War who came to know André Breton and Marcel Duchamp personally, "never ceases."[104]

In spite of many fertile relationships with fellow Surrealists—Wald and Zeller organized one group show and nine solo exhibitions for members of *Phases*—Wald felt apart from them because they were not open to her growing feminism. In a letter to me, she wrote: "When I first joined the *Phases* Movement and visited the Surrealists living in Paris, I was scolded for a feminist observation in my discourse. So my present feminist activity in the arts and in my writing is a break from the traditional Surrealist dogmas. I can accept no dogmas." Several years later, she describes such an incident to me again, etching its effect on her as even more severe. Referring to "orthodox Surrealists" and their response to her feminism, she told me in a telephone conversation: "In this I've found resistance. They ostracized me."[105]

Feminist Transformative Art

One theme emerging from Wald's feminism, the challenging of conventional women's roles, is expressed in a successful series of paintings from 1982–1988 called *The Wives*. Of three Surrealist women artists who wound up living and working in Mexico—Susana Wald, Leonora Carrington, and Remedios Varo—only Wald was not actually "displaced" by mainstream Surrealists because of being a wife.[106]

Leonora Carrington, who was married to painter Max Ernst, and Remedios Varo, married to poet Benjamin Péret, were both considered "wives of" instead of artists in their own right. Though Wald was coupled with Zeller, she was not considered an "initiate" of Surrealism but a practitioner because she was part of the collaborative and international "Surrealizing" moment, according to art historian Macarena Bravo-Cox. Bravo-Cox interviewed Wald for her scholarly study of Surrealist women artists in Mexico and found that Wald understood completely the devaluation and invisibility attributed to wives.[107]

Wald's series of paintings *Wives* captures and critiques that invisibility she understood as a woman. Perhaps her keen sensitivity to inconspicuousness was also heightened by her years of invisibility as a Jew. Wald belonged to what art critic Xavière Gauthier called in the 1970s an

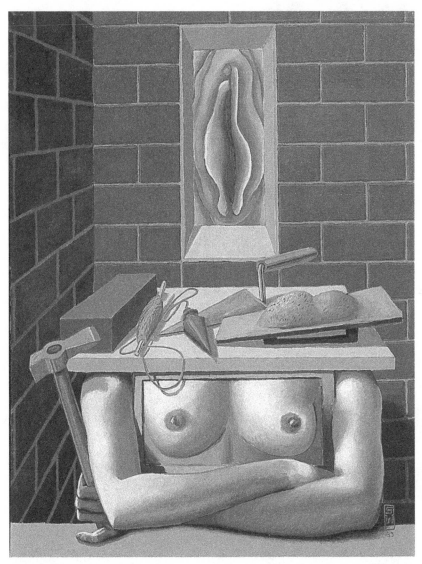

The Bricklayer's Wife

"aesthetic of surrealist perversion," an aesthetic of "femalitude." "Femalitude" was an assertion of essential female power, equivalent to male power, but essentially different. It challenged the male-constructed term *femininity* that associated the female with a weakened, adjunct status. Wald's "femalitude" held the promise of challenging patriarchal dominance.[108]

At first the *Wives* paintings seemed like a "fantastic joke" to Wald, what Freud called "parapraxis," and what we know as a Freudian slip. The

The Potter's Wife

paintings reveal that feminism was working through her unconscious. Her *Wives* re-interpreted from a woman's perspective the conception of the Great Mother she had found in Erich Neumann's study of the female archetype.[109]

In Neumann, the central symbolism of the feminine archetype is the vessel, or pot, that he equates with the woman's body. The woman's body becomes a vessel that nurtures the creative function. In Wald's paintings, on the other hand, wives are conceived as pieces of furniture endowed with women's body parts, and as bare-breasted torsos, many without heads. They are surrealist incongruities, jokes with serious implications.[110]

Wald realized after having finished *The Potter's Wife*, one painting in the series, that "she had painted the Great Mother, as described by Erich Neumann." But her unconscious had reworked the vessel, Neumann's symbol for the female archetype, in order to reappropriate and change it.[111]

In Wald's painting, the wife is figured as a large ceramic pot sitting on a potter's wheel. The pot is shaped like a female form with many bare breasts and no head, in the act of taking a coffee break. This wife is serving the artistic creativity of her husband as both muse and sculpted object. But in taking a coffee break, even without her head, she shows she is a "self" apart from her supportive functions. The viewer is made conscious of the wife as being more than the mindless position in which she has been placed. Thus, Wald's version of Neumann's symbol becomes a critique of it. This painting was selected for the prestigious XLII Venice Biennial of 1986.[112]

Conceiving wives in other paintings in the series as pieces of furniture, as seats, chairs, or "chests" of drawers, Wald shows the role of wives as their husbands' unending supports, providing for their every need. The wives are not themselves the active agents. Several of them are, like *The Potter's Wife*, headless, or they have humorous heads affixed to them: two hands holding a musician's bow—the musician's wife; a vulva engraved in the wall atop the "shoulders" of the bricklayer's wife; an upside-down woman's head framed in an old-fashioned camera for the photographer's wife.[113]

It seems clear that Wald's highly original interpretations of the wives—not only of the potter, but also of the fishmonger, the glass cutter, the musician, the art collector, and others who reflect different economic classes and occupations—challenge rather than reproduce male definitions/projections of the female archetype. These paintings reflect the widespread critique of conventional women's roles in patriarchal relationships that characterized the second-wave feminist movement in the Americas and Europe as a whole.

Another of the paintings in the *Wives'* series, *The Sorcerer's Wife*, gives shape to Wald's comment, written years later in her memoir *Windows*, "that there can be many eyes on one face, one façade."[114] In *The Sorcerer's Wife*, two piercing eyes that stare frontally at the viewer are being held high in place by the wife's hands above her prone nude body. The hands suggest that the wife can affix other eyes at other times to the mysterious face in the background, camouflaged and hidden by swirls of colored brushstrokes. Who is that undefined woman waiting behind those temporary eyes? Who are the women hidden by centuries of patriarchal art and narrative?

By far, the symbol that recurs most frequently in Wald's art, first in her ceramics, then in different phases throughout her painting, is the egg. Beginning in 1964, she exhibited ceramic sculptures of large eggs, fifty centimeters tall. Then, in the 1970s she created a series of clay sculptures in Toronto that had eggs of various sorts sitting on round shapes like plates, mostly all of them painted white. Again in the 1980s and 1990s, eggs appear, this time in paintings, and they continue to appear sometimes alongside human figures, and later by themselves, abstracted and enlarged, egg landscapes and seascapes, as it were.

The image of the egg comes to her, she told Martha Mabey "in visions, sometimes in daydreams, sometimes inserted into things apparently unrelated or while falling asleep." She says she doesn't know exactly why she paints them, but conjectures that they relate to the collective unconscious and the archetype of the Great Mother. They are about life and death, with the egg signaling "resurrection, a new beginning." Because Wald places the symbolic egg image in surreal contexts— "inserted into things apparently unrelated"—they become larger than life, icons carrying the proportion of myth. They relate, she said, not only to personal renewal, but also to the renewal of humanity at a time when "life is in danger." The egg is a "way to protest the destruction all around us."[115]

From where else in Wald's experience, whether in her consciousness or unconscious, might the mysterious egg have been derived? Could the egg signifying renewal in Wald's unconscious mind have originated from the same ancient world where the feminine archetype emerged, the ancient world where a narrative of liberation from oppression also emerged, a myth of freedom from slavery and emancipation to a new and promised land where renewal would be possible? This narrative of renewal out of

Full Moon

bondage is retold each year at the time of Passover in Jewish households, with the egg on the Seder plate symbolizing the recurring renewal that is always possible, not only in nature, but in society as well. The egg symbolizes the promise that we can shed the shackles of oppression and choose freedom and empowerment on personal and social levels.

Midnight Picnic

Wald's daughter was married to a Jewish man whose parents were observant and held Seders regularly each spring for Passover. Wald, who maintains dual residency in Mexico and Canada, still joins her daughter and her daughter's former in-laws in Toronto. Wald admitted to me, though, that she feels her in-laws are uncomfortable with her clumsy observance of traditional Jewish rituals.[116]

Wald told her biographer, Martha Mabey, that the egg paintings originate "from a deeper stratum" than the *Wives*. "They are more a manifestation of something of which I am unaware."[117] Could it be that after decades of keeping her Jewish identity hidden, her surreal paintings of eggs represent the surfacing of a Jewish ritual symbol from her past that has rested deeply within her unconscious and which she has had difficulty accessing? Wald may still sense danger on an emotional level when rituals are performed that connect her to the precious Jewish core she has so carefully tried to protect.

Declaring Jewish Identity in Mexico

Wald told me that her move to Oaxaca, Mexico, in 1994 resulted from Zeller's initiative. Not so well-integrated into Canadian society, he wished to live in a Spanish-speaking environment. In Oaxaca, a city of about three hundred thousand set in the foothills of the Sierra Madre mountains and six or seven hours southeast of Mexico City by car, Zeller found intellectuals and artists with whom he could share values and ideas about art. He and Wald had begun making yearly visits there in 1988.[118]

The city itself is a center for art, craft, and significant Zapotec and Mixtec archaeological sites. Internationally known Oaxacan artists Rodolfo Morales, Rufino Tomayo, and Francisco Toledo generously contributed to the city's development as a leading art center. Zeller moved there at the end of 1992 before Wald was ready to leave Toronto. He convinced Wald to join him in Oaxaca a year or so later.[119]

Wald told me she made the move against her better judgment in order to accommodate her partner, thus causing her to experience enormous psychological disruption. Despite her many accomplishments, including her successful and multiple careers—in art, writing, and teaching—and her facility in languages (she speaks four languages fluently), she came to feel like a "co-dependent," though she was actually "the moneymaker" for her family. When Wald took up permanent residence Oaxaca, she felt her otherness as a woman artist was becoming even further compounded.[120]

The feeling of being an outsider had never left Wald, just as Gerda Lerner never lost the "underground mentality" she internalized after her family's victimization in Vienna under the Nazis. In Wald's case, "otherness" included her bundle of secrets, first as an "undercover" Jew hiding as a Catholic in Hungary, then as a foreigner in the habit of protecting her Jewish core with different "covers" in the Christian cultures of Argentina, Chile, and Canada. Those different "covers" were respectively the relatively short-lived cover of cultural assimilation in Buenos Aires, the cover of Surrealism in Santiago, and finally the cover of Surrealist feminist spirituality in Toronto and Oaxaca.

Wald's feelings of aloneness in Oaxaca were ever present. She told me during meetings of the writing group we both attended that "life for older women in Oaxaca is hard." It's not a place "for sissies." Women friends she made in Oaxaca were mainly foreign visitors who moved away.[121] I realized sadly that I myself fit into that category. What brought some consolation was the fact that several of these women friends continued their relationship with Wald, as I did, even if it meant long-distance communication.

One such woman, Martha Mabey, wrote the brief biography of Wald that appeared in the illustrated volume *Susana Wald: Celebration* (2003), published during the time Wald was attempting to expand the audience for her creative work in both Oaxaca and other parts of Mexico. Up until recently, Mabey continued writing to Wald and continued writing about her as a Surrealist artist. In 2011, during meetings of the writing group to which Wald and I belonged, Wald told me regretfully, "I should be living in both Toronto and Oaxaca, traveling back and forth . . . but I brought all my goods to Oaxaca. . . . I come from a high middle-class family but now I live as an artist, without silver, porcelain or good rugs that I adore. . . . It took me a long time to find my peace."

Before Zeller passed away in 2019, Wald thought her residence in Oaxaca would be permanent. Zeller's passing allowed Wald to take up dual residence in both Toronto and Oaxaca. But at that time in 1994, she was faced with a new factor that had been added to her sense of exclusions, that of economic class. She needed to build herself up anew in Oaxaca in many ways—economically, artistically, and spiritually.

Unlike the two other Latin cities where she had resided—Buenos Aires and Santiago—the city of Oaxaca had no trace of its past Jewish presence. In Buenos Aires, she and her first husband, José Hausner, had been part of a vibrant, though assimilated, Jewish communal culture.

In Santiago, too, she and Hausner were in contact with a nonobservant Jewish community.

Then, when Wald became partners with Zeller in Santiago, they were asked by the daughters of a prominent Jewish family, the Friedmans, to create their father's tombstone. Señor Friedman had been a city councillor in Santiago, a man who performed extraordinary deeds for many people. With the help of a rabbi, Wald and Zeller learned the requirements for properly etching the Mogen David and the relevant Hebrew letters and numbers onto his tombstone so that the Kabbalist prescription that would be read on the Day of Resurrection could be fulfilled. Such prescription is part of Kabbalah, the ancient mystical strand within Judaism, and was part of the traditional Jewish belief system in Santiago at the time.[122]

But in Oaxaca, the Jewish presence was invisible. It was one of the least likely of Mexican cities in which a Jew could feel free to express her or his Jewish identity. If Wald herself had needed to emigrate to Mexico to reconnect with her Jewish identity, she might have been better off choosing Mexico City—which, like Buenos Aires and Santiago, is a capital city. Mexico City, where the largest concentration of Jews in the country resides, is home to approximately forty to fifty thousand Jews. Indeed, some of Wald's Jewish friends fled to Mexico City from Chile in the radicalizing aftermath of Allende's victory.[123]

But in Oaxaca, 80 percent of whose residents are descendants of the indigenous Zapotec and Mixtec peoples, Jews have not resided since the demise, in the mid-eighteen hundreds, of *cochineal* production and export. *Cochineal* is a brilliant, natural red dye that Jewish merchants sold to Europe, Asia, and the Far East. In 2013 Wald told me, "There is no Jewish community in Oaxaca, no ten males to gather for Shabbos. There may be four or five Jewish males, but I don't know them."[124]

Though anti-Semitic attitudes are part and parcel of Mexican culture, given the country's deeply seated Catholicism, Oaxacan xenophobia results more from its mountainside community having lived in total isolation for thousands of years, due partly to its orography. When the Inquisition of the sixteenth century spread from Spain and Portugal to the New World, it came with virulence to the more northern parts of Mexico. There hidden Jews, the *Conversos*, were uncovered by the

Catholic Church and burned at the stake. In the northern parts of the country during the Holy Week of Easter, *Semana Santa*, effigies of Judas Iscariot are still blown up, exploded, and burned, as Mexican-Catholic tradition continues to hold Jews responsible for the death of Jesus.[125]

In Oaxaca, some traces of European Spanish/Catholic anti-Jewish bias appear more subtly in the culture's language. The Spanish dictionary defines a *judiada* as a "dirty trick, a cruel thing, or extortion," and a *ladino*, or Spanish Jew, is considered to be a person of mixed race who is "crafty."[126] In this context certain stereotypes of Jews remain in Oaxaca. My husband and I encountered these stereotypes during our eighteen winters in Oaxaca. When asking Oaxacans of modest means whom we befriended about the Jews in their city, we were told that the Jews were the wealthy bankers, for example, or that their families were concerned with frugality and wealth accumulation. It is understandable then that in Oaxaca, where there was no visible community of Jews, Wald would feel particularly vulnerable and cautious about protecting her core religious/ spiritual identity.

Slowly, Wald became fortified and inspired by her readings of Jung and Neumann in the 1990s. These supports helped her express her spiritual and aesthetic yearnings, rooted in her Jewish core, in the large mural she created on commission for the University of Michoacan (1994–5). Wald titled the work *Dazzling Light*. Its central image is that of Sofia, who represents wisdom, and according to Neumann, a many thousand years' process of spiritualization of the feminine archetype. Wald had studied the archetype Sofia as an early manifestation of the Shekinah, the feminine aspect of the Hebrew God.[127]

Wald's Sofia is presented as a floating female figure encircled by an expansive golden halo. Sofia may have heralded what Wald called a "new reality . . . emerging from the unconscious," a new reality for herself, and perhaps for women more generally. By painting her version of Sofia, Wald was once again gaining resilience and strength by encoding her Jewish core in a different iconic mythology. In the painting, other figures surround Sofia. They gesture in expressions of "admiration and worship." The mural appears on campus in the former Convent of Tiripetio.[128]

During that same time, Wald was also deriving income by painting portraits. The portraits contributed to her ability eventually to build a house for herself and Zeller in a native village close to Oaxaca. The house, which they designed, became their permanent Oaxaca home. In addition, Wald contracted to produce the book *Spanish for Dummies* (1999), a pragmatic venture which was an excursion of sorts from her aesthetic pursuits, though it did result from her undeniable expertise as a translator. The book's publication was highly successful and profitable for Wald. It spiraled in several different editions and types of publications.[129] These activities and others helped Wald reestablish her sense of personal rebirth.

While Wald was in process of restoring herself economically and professionally—teaching a course, writing an editorial every Saturday for *Noticias de Oaxaca*, and editing the manuscripts of others, in addition to creating her own art—political and economic realities in Oaxaca were becoming worse.

Economic conditions in Oaxaca had never been good. Despite the renown of the *city* of Oaxaca for the arts, the *state* of Oaxaca, of which the city is the capital, is one of the poorest in the country. More than 70 percent of Oaxaca's population lives in severe poverty, and more than half of the state's population earns less than the national minimum wage. Only half of the state's inhabitants "have access to basic services, such as electricity and running water and fewer than 40 percent of Oaxacans have the opportunity to study beyond elementary school."[130]

Over the course of decades, the failure of the ruling political party, the Institution Revolutionary Party (PRI), to address these vast inequities caused mounting discontent. Opposition rose to the state government's mismanagement, corruption, and abuses when it was alleged that the PRI candidate for governor, Ulises Ruiz, won the controversial election of 2004 through fraud, and then attempted to imprison his opponent who stood for reforms. By the end of 2006, when Ruiz was repressing popular mobilizations for change with particular harshness and authoritarianism, the massive conflict that came to be known as the "insurrection" took shape.[131]

The 2006 insurrection began on May 22 with a teachers' strike demanding higher wages. The teachers occupied several buildings and streets in the city of Oaxaca, a strategy they had used for two-and-a-half decades to gain small wage increases. Though in the past these strikes sometimes erupted in violence and caused some damage to downtown areas, normal activities would typically resume after a week or two.[132] This time it was different.

On June 14, the local police violently broke up one of the teachers' demonstrations in their attempt to repress the movement entirely. Protesters then expanded their demands to include the resignation of Governor Ruiz. This became a turning point, prompting the creation of the Popular Assembly of the Peoples of Oaxaca, or the APPO.[133]

Numerous civil and political organizations—human rights associations, agrarian movements, indigenous organizations, members of political parties, radical leftist groups, unions, students, women's groups—joined the teachers' movement to form the APPO. The APPO was also supported by some Oaxacan entrepreneurs and former governors. While the main stated objective of the APPO was the immediate resignation of Governor Ruiz, this movement also called for broader and long overdue economic and political transformations in the state. What began in May 2006 as an annual teachers' demonstration for better pay quickly escalated into full-fledged civil unrest.[134]

The movement shut down Oaxaca's downtown for five months, prevented around 1.3 million students from attending classes for months, and left about twenty people dead. The conflict ultimately reached national dimensions bringing many polarized sides face-to-face: paramilitary forces, guerrilla groups, Marxists, resentful and out-of-favor politicians, and the Church. In order to regain control of the capital city, then-President Vicente Fox, in his final month in office, ordered the intervention of the federal riot police.[135]

One unprecedented feature of this insurrection keeping it vital and alive was its takeover of communication media. Throughout Oaxaca's history, communication media had been controlled by local government authorities or locals in collusion with them. But in the insurrection of 2006, popular forces took over key local communication media and, for the first time in Oaxaca's history, utilized them for organizational purposes.

The APPO took over several radio stations, as well as the official local TV channel (channel 9). These events consolidated and strengthened the movement. Journalist Diego Enrique Osorno observed:

> For the first time in Oaxaca's history, "real" Oaxacan men and women appeared on TV expressing the peoples' demands. This

fact contributed to incorporate further citizens into the APPO movement. TV worked as mirror, where "people" saw themselves reflected on, and thus felt identified with the movement and decided to participate.[136]

It was in this context of asking local leaders to participate in the movement that Wald was invited to speak during the uprising. She had been so affected by the succession of events that she couldn't continue her visual work as a painter. She was spurred to write a book in Spanish, *Nueve Lunas* (Nine Moons), that mixed early events in her life with the uprising. Moreover, she had been participating in a two-hour weekly public radio program that Governor Ruiz canceled.[137]

Wald felt compelled to speak. In spite of political danger, and her past history of protecting her Jewish core identity, she believed that revealing previously hidden parts of herself could inspire the intellectuals who were trying to keep going. She addressed a gathering of about three hundred people. She read her own text as a literary piece or short essay about being Jewish and the importance of surviving under oppressive regimes. She hoped to encourage the continuation of the movement and from her own experience relate how the powerless can empower themselves by gaining strength from one another. It was a landmark event for Wald. She told me, "It has only been in 2006 that I have said publicly that I am Jewish. It took me that long."[138] Later in her correspondence to me she wrote:

> I had noticed that the persecution (my phone line was tapped—people disappeared) affected me in ways beyond reason. I searched for some explanation. I found it in the cloud of terror my elders experienced in face of events during the Second World War that I lived under and which I could not understand as a child. I stated something to the effect that I was concerned about the persecutions that I was witnessing, saying that I had also been persecuted because of my being Jewish.[139]

This public declaration seemed to be part of Wald's own personal empowerment process, her way of finally moving her "otherness," her outsider status, out of the shadows and owning it as part of her full identity.

After delivering her speech, the editor-in-chief of the popular daily *Noticias de Oaxaca*, which had also suffered attacks from Governor Ruiz, invited Wald to write a column for the paper. These were Wald's Saturday editorials, for which she later became known.[140]

In writing her late-life memoir *Life Matters: Windows*, Wald continued the process of reintegrating her Jewish identity into her personal history. Wald's shadow-counterpart, Agnes, who helped Wald preserve her Jewishness when she converted to Catholicism, also helps Wald see relationships between the practice of Surrealism and Wald's Jewish identity. Agnes explains that Breton, Surrealism's founder, wanted Surrealism to be "free," that is, to be liberated from "the stifling influence, the retrograde ideas of the church," to be free from "commercial enterprises" and from "political and psychological constraints imposed by totalitarian organizations." Subtly, Wald begins to connect Surrealism's concept of individual freedom with the outsider status as a Jew she has experienced over her lifetime beginning with the Nazi-takeover in Hungary.

Early in *Windows*, Agnes tells Wald:

"From early on I know I'm Jewish. This condition is mixed with the fear that dominates my childhood. . . I'm conscious of the fact that I'm an outsider. . . . . Being an outsider is the most persistent feature of my life. . . People I meet in all countries that I live in consider me a foreigner in one way or another."

And Wald responds to Agnes: "There are good aspects to this: the outsider is free to be loyal to groups and ideas of her choice."[141]

This empowering insight expresses how closely Wald's view of the outsider resonates with a Jewish perspective on liberation and human rights. As the Exodus narrative illustrates, to be free, the individual must shake off the shackles of oppression and exercise choice to follow a different path. The outsider may actually be in a better position than the insider to evaluate shortcomings in dominant systems and may therefore be more able to chart new and improved courses that could or should be taken.

As both a Jew and a Surrealist, Wald experienced the ways repressive political, economic, and religious institutions blunted people's perceptions of their human rights, needs, and desires. As an artist and spiritual

seeker, she sought freedom to satisfy a "common, universal need of transcendence," a need she personally fulfilled with the help of rituals. Practicing rituals of choice also required freedom. In *Windows,* Agnes tells
Wald that among Surrealists, whether rituals are considered "religious,"
"sexual," or "magic," they all "are signs of deep-rooted human needs."[142]

Interestingly, when Agnes goes further to explain the function of
rituals from the Surrealist perspective, she sounds surprisingly rabbinic,
as when rabbis explain the Jewish ritual of daily blessings. Both Surrealism and Judaism attempt to elevate the individual's perception of
everyday reality to the level of the miraculous: Agnes says, "Rituals turn
the commonplace into the transcendent" and bring the ordinary "into
the realm of the marvelous. That is the beauty the innocent child that I
am enjoys from the beginning." The "beginning" to which Agnes refers
is most likely the childhood they both shared, when they both knew
from early on that they were Jewish and when Agnes/Wald observed
her mother lighting candles "when she remembered the dead among her
own relations."[143] But as Wald's life has time and again demonstrated,
discriminatory, and sometimes genocidal, politics restricted her freedom
to practice rituals, whether they expressed Surrealist concepts or Jewish,
religious/spiritual identity.

At this point in the memoir, Wald responds to Agnes by saying:

> "For most of my life I don't want to lie when I'm asked if I'm
> Jewish. And I don't want to tell the truth. In 2006 I finally come
> out by reading in a public event in Oaxaca an essay about the
> repression of the Indigenous peoples. I then say that I know the
> feeling because I also have been persecuted for being Jewish. Yet
> the person leading the event finds that I shouldn't have done it.
> He's trying to protect me, as that confessor did in Budapest. . . .
> In Mexico, probably the most xenophobic country I ever lived in,
> being Jewish could be a handicap."[144]

The section moves to conclusion with Wald enumerating all the other
reasons she's been relegated to outsider status and marginalized in the
different countries she's resided: her language, her culture, her female
gender as writer and artist.[145] Yet her earlier words about being a *Jewish*
outsider show that Jewish identity has also offered her the empowerment

that derives from the belief in freedom of choice: the Jew as outsider is "free to be loyal to groups and ideas of her choice." Outsider status is thereby transformed and recreated as the freedom to be different, to choose roads not taken.

During her lifetime, Wald took on the protective cover of other "outsider" groups—first Catholics, then Surrealists—because since childhood, having internalized the Nazi threat to annihilate Jews, she needed a "buffer" identity. However, these other "covers" she assumed were not risk-free, since she lived under subsequent totalitarian regimes that repressed groups that challenged their authority. Nevertheless, as an artist she required freedom to express her creative self, and she found common ground between her core identity as Jew and her other affiliations. She remained a risk-taker, though, never comfortable with required conformity. When Catholicism and mainstream Surrealism became too dogmatic and restrictive, too threatening of her freedom and artistic creativity, she broke away, becoming an outsider once again.

As perennial outsider, Wald resembles most that figure in Jewish tradition of the archetypal nonconformist, the one who chooses a path forever different from that of the mainstream. In Jewish tradition, that archetype can be represented by the founding patriarch Abraham (as well as his progeny Isaac and Jacob), to whom Moses refers when in Deuteronomy 26:5, he says, "My father was a fugitive Aramean." They were homeless fugitives from Aramea (Aram) whose people became enslaved in Egypt, but who were brought to freedom by following the voice of God, pathfinders who sought and found contact with the transcendent. Like these spiritual predecessors, Wald has *stood apart* as outsider, and has *stood for the right to choose to be different*.

Notes

1. The first treatment in English of Wald's work as a Surrealist appeared in 2003, with an introduction "Susana Wald" by Martha Mabey, *Susana Wald: Celebration* (Oaxaca, Mexico: El colegio de Oaxaca, 2003), 16–29. With internet translations into English, the writings of scholar Macarena Bravo-Cox have expanded Wald's audience, as in Macarena Bravo-Cox "Susana Wald: The Woman

of Herself" ("Susana Wald: La mujer de sí misma"), Agulha Revista de Cultura 1999–2020, Arc Edições/Uma Agulha em todo o mundo, Friday August 26, 2019, which is based on her master's thesis on feminist Surrealist artists at Ecoles des Hautes en sciences sociales del artes con magister en artes y lenguajes, Paris, France, 2015–17. The thesis gained Aesthetic Mention. Portions of this thesis referenced and quoted in this chapter are translated from the French by Dr. Thomas Petruso.

2. Diana Denham & C.A.S.A Collective, eds., *Teaching Rebellion: Stories from the Grassroots Mobilization in Oaxaca* (Oakland, California: PM Press, 2008). I also have private email correspondence from Kate Sherman on-site in Oaxaca "OAX: The New Threat," October 14, 2006.

3. Milton Teichman and Sharon Leder, eds., *Truth and Lamentation: Stories and Poems on the Holocaust* (Urbana and Chicago: University of Illinois Press, 1998); Leder and Teichman, eds., *The Burdens of History: Post-Holocaust Generations in Dialogue* (Merion, Pennsylvania: Merion Westfield Press International, 2000).

4. My interviews with Susana Wald took place at Villas de Alcalá, 1005 Calle Macedonio Alcalá, Oaxaca, Mexico, January–February 2012–13, 2016–17.

5. Interview with Wald, Oaxaca, 2013. See Mabey "Susana Wald," 28, and see the Timeline in *Susana Wald: Celebration*, 82-84. Also Susana Wald, "Winter, 1970—The Surrealism in Chile exhibition," *Life Matters: Windows*, unpublished memoir (2013–17), 45–49.

6. Interview with Wald, Oaxaca, 2013.

7. Wald, *Life Matters: Windows*, 37.

8. Some of these principles, such as the unlocking of the subconscious, the subjectivity of time, and the juxtaposition of unlikely and incongruous images, are clearly explained in Anna Claybourne's *Surrealism* (Chicago: Heinemann Library, 2009).

9. Wald's artistic and literary achievements from 1968 until 2003, including translations, are enumerated in the Timeline in *Susana Wald: Celebration*, 82–102, including her commission in 1999 to write the bestselling *Spanish for Dummies* (Hoboken, New Jersey, 1999) for Berlitz and IDG Books. See this chapter, 78–79. In addition, she

wrote *Tres grandes poemas de Enjeduena dedicados a Inana* (Mexico: UACM, Difusión Cultural y Extensión Universitaria, 2009), a translation into Spanish of Betty De Shong Meador's *Inanna, Lady of the Largest Heart* (Austin, Texas: University of Texas Press, 2001). See this chapter, 70. See also this chapter for Wald's volume *Nueve Lunas* (Nine Moons), 81; and for her editorial columns for *Noticias de Oaxaca*, 79, 81. Google searches of Susana Wald yield notices of her many exhibits in Toronto, several Mexico locations and other international locations, and of numerous articles about her.

10. See Note 9.
11. See Note 8.
12. See Note 9. For access to Zeller Wald archive, University of Talca: Eduardo Bravo Pezoa, edbravo@utalca.cl
13. See Timeline, "Exposiciones," *Susana Wald: Celebration*, 98–102.
14. Mabey, "Susana Wald," 20-21 and *Susana Wald: Celebration*, 33–34, 43, 82.
15. The blogspot of Joanne Arnott "Susana Wald: Voyage to the Bottom" (Friday, February 1, 2013) illustrates one example of how the literary and artistic works of Susana Wald broaden understanding of feminist Surrealism for an English-speaking author/artist; joannearnott.blogspot.com/2013/02/Susana-wald-voyage-to-the-bottom.html See also Note 1.
16. *Susana Wald: Celebration*, 16. Also Wald, *Life Matters: Windows*, 13.
17. See preface, Note 6. The persistence of this conflation is reflected, for example, in several recent publications: Robert Rockaway, "Introduction: The Jew as 'Other' in America," *Jewish History* (Baltimore, Maryland: John Hopkins University Press, December 2001) Vol. 89 Number 4: 353–545; Andrei Oisteanu, *Inventing the Jew: Antisemitic Stereotypes in Romania and Other Central-East European Cultures* (Lincoln, Nebraska: University of Nebraska Press, 2009); Manuela and Vivian Liska, *Sartre, Jews, and the Other: Rethinking Anstisemitism, Race, and Gender* (Oldenburg, Germany: De Gruyter Oldenbourg, 2020).
18. David Meyer, "Anti-Semitism in Europe: Jews Are Outsiders, Not Equals," *Haaretz*, March 3, 2013; https://www.haaretz.com/opinion/.premium-david-meyer-jews-still-on-european-fringe-1.5232403.

19. Interview with Wald, Oaxaca, 2013.

20. Ibid.

21. Mabey, "Susana Wald," 16, italics added.

22. Interview with Wald, Oaxaca, 2013.

23. Ibid. See also Wald, *Life Matters: Windows*. 14.

24. Ibid.

25. David. B. Green, "This Day in Jewish History/Hungary Enacts First Jewish Law," *Haaretz*, May 29, 2014; https://www.haaretz.com/jewish/.premium-this-day-hungary-enacts-first-anti-jewish-law-1.5250019.

26. Interview with Wald, Oaxaca, 2013.

27. Interviews with Wald, Oaxaca, 2016–17.

28. Ivana Nikolic, "Last Survivors Recall WWII Massacre in Occupied Yugoslavia," *Balkan Transitional Justice*, January 23, 2019; https://balkaninsight.com/2019/01/23/last-survivors-recall-wwii-massacre-in-occupied-yugoslavia-01-22-2019/. See also Árpád von Klimó, "Introduction," *Remembering Cold Days: The 1942 Massacre of Novi Sad, Hungarian Politics and Society 1942–1989* (Pittsburgh, Penn.: University of Pittsburgh Press, 2018), 3–12; and Interview with Wald, Oaxaca, 2013.

29. Interview with Wald, Oaxaca, 2013.

30. Ibid. See also Dr. Robert Rozett, "Conscripted Slaves: Hungarian Jewish Forced Laborers on the Eastern Front During World War II," *Yad Vashem*; https://www.yadvashem.org/articles/general/conscripted-slaves-hungarian-jewish-forced-laborers.html and "Hungarian Labor Service Battalions," *Geni*; https://www.geni.com/projects/Hungarian-Labor-Service-Battalions/14800.

31. Livia Bitton Jackson, "Somarja: March 28, 1944, "*I Have Lived a Thousand Years: Growing Up in the Holocaust* (New York: Simon and Schuster, 1997), 30. Confirmed in www.history.com/topics/world-war-ii/the-holocaust/pictures/remembering-the-holocaust-/hungarian-jews-wearing-yellow-stars.

32. Interview with Wald, Oaxaca, 2013.

33. Interviews with Wald, Oaxaca, 2016–17. See also Wald, *Life Matters: Windows*, 50.

34. "Raoul Wallenberg and the Rescue of Jews in Budapest," *United States Holocaust Memorial Museum Holocaust Encyclopedia*;

encyclopedia.ushmm.org/content/en/article/raoul-wallenberg-and-the-rescue-of-jews-in-budapest. Also see the editors of *Encyclopedia Britannica*, "Raoul Wallenberg: Swedish Diplomat," *Encyclopedia Britannica*; britannica.com/biography/Raoul-Wallenberg.

35. "Raoul Wallenberg: Rescue of Hungarian Jews." *Jewish Virtual Library: A Project of AICE*; jewishvirtuallibrary.org/raoul-wallenberg-2.

36. "Budapest," *United States Holocaust Memorial Museum Holocaust Encyclopedia*; encyclopedia.ushmm.org/content/en/article/Budapest.

37. "Raoul Wallenberg: Rescue of Hungarian Jews," *Jewish Virtual Library: A Project of AICE*.

38. Wald's letter is attached to her email message to me, September 7, 2017. Also her "intervention" revising my draft of February 21, 2017, states that Wallenberg's signature appears on the *shcutzpass* (document) that her mother used to secure her father's release from conscripted labor.

39. See Dr. Robert Rosett, "Conscripted Slaves . . .", *Yad Vashem*.

40. Interviews with Wald, Oaxaca, 2016–17.

41. Ibid.

42. Ibid.

43. Wald, *Life Matters: Windows*, 5–6, italics added.

44. "Raoul Wallenberg and the Rescue of Jews in Budapest," *United States Holocaust Memorial Museum Holocaust Encyclopedia* and "Raoul Wallenberg: Rescue of Hungarian Jews." *Jewish Virtual Library: A Project of AICE*.

45. "Hungary-Postwar Hungary," http://countrystudies.us/hungary/36.htm and Interview with Wald, Oaxaca, 2017.

46. Wald, *Life Matters: Windows*, 35.

47. Ibid., 10.

48. Ibid., 11.

49. Ibid., 3.

50. Ibid., 11.

51. Ibid., 12–14.

52. Ibid., 3.

53. Ibid., 11–12.

54. Alice Rethinger Watson, "The Life and 'Crimes' of Cardinal Mindszenty," *Catholic Culture*; https://www.catholicculture.org/culture/library/view.cfm?recnum=661.

55. Ibid. See also "This Day in History, February 8, 1949, Cardinal Mindszenty of Hungary Sentenced," *History*; https://www.history.com/this-day-in-history/cardinal-mindszenty-of-hungary-sentenced.

56. Wald, *Life Matters: Windows*, 7, 11.

57. "Hungary in the Soviet Orbit," *Encyclopedia Britannica*; https://www.britannica.com/place/Hungary/Hungary-in-the-Soviet-orbit.

58. Interview with Wald, Oaxaca, 2013 and Wald, *Life Matters: Windows*, 11.

59. Interviews with Wald, Oaxaca, 2016–17.

60. Wald, *Life Matters: Windows*, 14.

61. Ibid., 12.

62. Ibid., 45.

63. Interviews with Wald, Oaxaca, 2016–17; Wald, *Life Matters: Windows*, 44.

64. Interviews with Wald, Oaxaca, 2016–17.

65. Ibid.

66. Ibid. See also Wald, *Life Matters: Windows*, 20–21, 41–43.

67. Wald, *Life Matters:Windows*, 12. Interviews with Wald, Oaxaca, 2016–17.

68. Wald, *Life Matters: Windows*, 12–13.

69. Interviews with Wald, Oaxaca, 2016–17.

70. Ibid.

71. Ludwig Zeller, "Afterword by the Author," *To Saw the Beloved Only When Necessary*. Translated into English by Susana Wald, Beatriz Zeller, A.F. Moritz, Robin Skelton (Toronto: Exile Editions, 1990) 101.

72. Interviews with Wald, Oaxaca, 2016–17 for Zeller's family background and his early research into Romanticism. See also the "Introduction" to Ludwig Zeller's *The Rules of the Game: Selected Shorter Poems 1952–2008* (Toronto, Ontario: Quattro Books, 2012) by A.F. Moritz, Zeller's translator. In my correspondence with Wald 2017–18, Wald adds to Moritz's discussion of Zeller's

attraction to Surrealism by referring me to the influence of
Huidobro and Pellegrini on Zeller.

73. Douglas Messerli, "La Mandrágora (The Mandrake) group," *The
Pip (Project for Innovative Poetry) Blog*, July 1, 2011; http://pippo-
etry.blogspot.com/2011/07/la-mandragora-mandrake.html Please
note that Messerli incorrectly names Zeller's wife "Beatriz" Zeller.
Beatriz is in fact the step-daughter of Zeller and his wife who is
Susana Wald, Beatriz's mother. Also Wald's correspondence to
me (2017–18) discusses how she and Zeller shepherded the second
generation of Surrealists in Chile. For the broad reach of Huidobro,
see *The Origins of Vicente Huidobro's 'Creacionismo' (1911–1916) and
Its Evolution (1917–1947)* by Luisa M. Perdigó (New York: Mellen,
1994), Bruce Dean Willis, "Preface," *Aesthetics of Equilibrium: The
Vanguard Poetics of Vicente Huidobro and Mário de Andrade* (West
Lafayette, Indiana: Purdue University Press, 2006), xvi–xviii; and
https://www.brittanica.com/biography/Vicente Huidobro.

74. John Joseph Lyons, "Aldo Pellegrini: The Subversive Effect of
Poetry," *Johnjosephlyons*; https://johnjosephlyons.com/2020/03/31/
aldo-pellegrini-the-subversive-effect-of-poetry/. See also Melanie
Nicholson, *Surrealism in Latin American Literature: Searching for
Breton's Ghost* (New York: Palgrave Macmillan, 2013), especially
"Argentina's Pioneer Surrealists," 47–57 and "Chile: The Avatars
and the Antagonists of La Mandrágora," 175–201.

75. André Breton, *Manifesto of Surrealism*, 1924; https://www.tcf.
ua.edu/Classes/Jbutler/T340/SurManifesto/ManifestoOfSur-
realism.htm.

76. Brenton Sanderson, "Tristan Tzara and the Jewish Roots of
Dada, Part 1," *Occidental Observer*, November 15, 2011; www.
theoccidentalobserver.net/2011/11/15/tristan-tzara-and-the-
jewish-roots-of-dada-part-1/.

77. Interviews with Wald, Oaxaca, 2016–17.

78. Ibid.; *Les Règles del Juego* [The Rules of the Game] (Santiago, Chile:
Ediciones Casa de la Luna, 1968); *Susana Wald: Celebration*, 82.

79. Interviews with Wald, Oaxaca. 2016-17.

80. Katherine Conley, Review of *Surrealism and The Politics of Eros,
1938–1968* by Alyce Mahon (London: Thames & Hudson, 2005).

In *French Forum*, Vol. 31, No.3 (University of Pennsylvania Press, Fall 2006), 168–170.

81. *Susana Wald: Celebration*, 82.

82. The Editors of *Encyclopedia Britannica*, "Salvador Allende Gossens," britannica.com/biography/Salvador/Allende, updated June 22, 2020; Juan de Onis, "Allende, Chilean Marxist, Wins Vote for Presidency," *New York Times Archive*, September 6, 1970, https://www.nytimes.com/1970/09/06/archives/allende-chilean-marxist-wins-vote-for-presidency-allende-chilean.html; Joseph Novitski, "Allende, Marxist Leader, Elected Chile's President," *New York Times Archive*, October 25, 1970, https://www.nytimes.com/1970/10/25/archives/allende-marxist-leader-elected-chiles-president-allende-elected.html.

83. History.com editors, "Chilean President Salvador Allende Dies in Coup," *History*, https://www.history.com/this-day-in-history/allende-dies-in-coup, July 23, 2020, and "Chile Buries General as Martyr," *New York Times Archive*, October 27, 1970, https://www.nytimes.com/1970/10/27/archives/chile-buries-general-as-martyr.html.

84. Interview with Wald, Oaxaca, 2013. See also Note 5.

85. Wald, "Winter, 1970—The Surrealism in Chile Exhibition," *Life Matters: Windows*, 46, 48.

86. Ibid., 47.

87. Ibid., 46–47.

88. Interviews with Wald, Oaxaca, 2016–17.

89. Ibid.

90. *Wald, Life Matters: Windows*, 52.

91. Wald's break from *Phases* over feminism appears in her email attachment to her message to me of September 7, 2017. Wald's comments on Dorothea Tanning and Remedios Varo, "Art Collecting," *Life Matters: Windows*, 27–28. See discussions of Wald in relation to these women artists in Macarena Bravo-Cox's master's thesis on feminist Surrealist artists, 79–91 and 102–107 (see Note 1). See also Charlotte Higgins, "Leonora Carrington: Wild at Heart," *The Guardian*, January 25, 2015, https://www.theguardian.com/artanddesign/2015/jan/28/leonara-carrington-wild-at-heart;

Lexi Manatakis, "Seven Female Artists Who Subverted Surrealism," *Dazed*, April 2019, https://www.dazeddigital.com/art-photography/article/43833/1/seven-female-artists-who-subverted-surrealism-dorothea-tanning-tate-modern, and Stefan Van Raay, Joanna Moorhead, Teresa Arcq, *Surreal Friends: Leonora Carrington, Remedios Varo and Kati Horna* (London: Lund Humphries, 2010).

92. Interviews with Wald, Oaxaca, 2016–17.

93. Margot Adler, "Inner Space: The Spiritual Frontier" (feminist.com, 2003), www.feminist.com/resources/artspeech/insp/inner.html

94. Robert S. Short, "The Politics of Surrealism 1920–36," *Journal of Contemporary History:* Vol. 1, No. 2, "Left-Wing Intellectuals Between the Wars" (London: Sage Publications, Ltd., 1966), 3–25; https://www.jstor.org/stable/259920?seq=1.

95. Ibid., 14–25.

96. Ibid., 8.

97. Ibid., 3–6 and Interview with Wald, Oaxaca, 2013. See also André Breton and Diego Rivera, "Manifesto for a Revolutionary Independent Art, 1938," *Marxist Literary Criticism*, 2001, https://www.marxists.org/subject/art/lit_crit/works/rivera/manifesto.htm. It is believed that Breton wrote the Manifesto with Leon Trotsky, although it was signed by Diego Rivera.

98. Interviews with Wald, Oaxaca, 2016–17.

99. Patricia Allmer, *Angels of Anarchy: Women Artists and Surrealism* (Munich: Prestel Publishing, 2009) and "Feminist Interventions: Revising the Canon" in David Hopkins, ed., *A Companion to Dada and Surrealism* (Hoboken, New Jersey: John Wiley & Sons, Inc., 2016), 366–81.

100. Erich Neumann, *The Great Mother: Analysis of the Archetype,* translated by Ralph Manheim (Princeton, New Jersey: Princeton University Press, 1955). Also Lance S. Owens, "C.J. Jung and Erich Neumann: The Zaddik, Sophia and the Shekinah," *Psychological Perspectives: A Quarterly Journal of Jungian Thought,* 61:2, 2018; https://www.academia.edu/31768301/C._G._Jung_and_Erich_Neumann_The_Zaddik_Sophia_and_the_Shekinah_2016_2018_

and Sophia Compton, "Evolution of an Archetype: Emergence of the Feminine Shekinah," *Academia,* 1-18; https://www.academia.edu/29077353/Evolution_of_an_Archetype_Emergence_of_the_Feminine_Shekinah. Excerpt from chapter 2 of *The Transcendent Feminine: Shekinah Glory, From Theophany to Theosophy* by Madonna S. Compton (Create Space Independent Publishing Platform, 2013).

101. See Note 9. Interview with Wald, Oaxaca, 2013.

102. Judy Grahn, "Foreword: Enheduanna's Forty-Fourth Century," *Inanna, Lady of the Largest Heart* by Betty De Shong Meador, xvi and xi-xv, and Meador's "Part I The Cultural and Historical Context," 3–9.

103. Wald, *Life Matters: Windows,* insert mailed to me, 2016–17, 1–2; Susan L. Power, "Surrealist Intrusion and Disenchantment on Madison Avenue, 1960," *Networking Surrealism in the USA. Agents, artists, and the market,* 435, 437; https://books.ub.uni-heidelberg.de/arthistoricum/reader/download/485/485-17-87215-1-10-20191209.pdf and *The Eugenio Granell Foundation,* http://www.eugeniogranell.org/eugenio-granell.

104. Wald, *Life Matters: Windows,* insert, 2–3 and *The Eugenio Granell Foundation.*

105. Wald's break from *Phases* first mentioned, see Note 91. On January 11, 2019, Wald refers again to being ostracized by *Phases* in a telephone conversation about this chapter.

106. Bravo Cox, master's thesis on feminist Surrealist artists, 107.

107. Ibid., 102–103.

108. Ibid., 106–107.

109. Ibid., 102–104.

110. Jacques Schnier, "Erich Neumann, The Great Mother: An Analysis of the Archetype," *College Art Journal,* Vol. 16, Issue 1, 1956, 78–80; https://www.tandfonline.com/doi/abs/10.1080/15436322.1956.11466169?journalCode=rcaj19 and Bravo-Cox, master's thesis on feminist surrealist artists, 102–105.

111. Mabey, "Susana Wald," 27.

112. Ibid. and *Susana Wald: Celebration,* 54.

113. *Susana Wald: Celebration,* 52–55.

114. Wald, *Life Matters: Windows*, 3.

115. Mabey, "Susana Wald," 25–26.

116. Interview with Wald, Oaxaca, 2013

117. Mabey, "Susana Wald," 27.

118. *Susana Wald: Celebration*, 92.

119. Interview with Wald, Oaxaca, 2013.

120. Ibid.

121. Ibid.

122. Interviews with Wald, Oaxaca, 2016–17.

123. World Jewish Congress (WJC), https://www.worldjewishcongress. org/en/about/communities/MX; Interviews with Wald, Oaxaca, 2016–17.

124. Alvin and Arlene Starkman, "Not a Jew to Be Found?" *Casa Machaya, Oaxaca Bed and Breakfast*, http://www.oaxacadream.com/ articles/academic4.html; interview with Wald, Oaxaca, 2013.

125. Haim F. Ghiuzeli, "Crypto-Jews in Mexico during Spanish Colonial Era," *Museum of the Jewish People at Beit Hatfutsot*, https:// www.bh.org.il/visit-us/general-information/; Personal visits to San Miguel de Allende, Mexico during Semana Santa, 2001–2017.

126. SpanishDict, https://www.spanishdict.com/translate/ judiada#:~:text=report%20this%20ad-,judiada,Word%20Forms.

127. See Note 100.

128. Mabey, "Susana Wald," 28–29; *Susana Wald: Celebration*, 63.

129. Susana Wald, *Spanish for Dummies* (Hoboken, New Jersey: Wiley Publishing, 1999), *Spanish Phrases for Dummies* (Hoboken, New Jersey: Wiley Publishing, 2004); *Daily Spanish for Dummies: Mini Edition* (Hoboken, New Jersey: Wiley Publishing, 2010); online version 2011, CD, and other iterations.

130. Diana Denham & C.A.S.A Collective, eds. *Teaching Rebellion: Stories from the Grassroots Mobilization in Oaxaca*, 27.

131. Guadalupe Correa-Cabrera, "Political Factionalism in Southern Mexico: The Case of Oaxaca 2006," *Journal of Politics in Latin America* 4, 1 [1/2012], 93–96.

132. Ibid., 91–92.

133. Ibid.

134. Ibid.

135. Ibid.

136. Ibid., 97.

137. Telephone conversation with Wald, January 11, 2019.

138. Ibid.

139. Email correspondence from Wald, February 9, 2019.

140. Ibid.

141. Wald, *Life Matters: Windows*, 12–14.

142. Ibid., 13.

143. Ibid., 14.

144. Ibid., 13–14.

145. Ibid., 14.

3

RUTH W. MESSINGER (NOVEMBER 6, 1940–) AND SOCIAL JUSTICE JUDAISM

Personal Association

I first heard about the American Jewish World Service (AJWS) during my early visits to San Miguel de Allende, Mexico (2001–2003). A Jewish couple my husband and I met, Stan and Marcia Klein, tourists like ourselves, were jubilant. They had spent time working for what they called the "Jewish Peace Corps." They had just arrived in Mexico after volunteering for AJWS in its Volunteer Corps, first in Zimbabwe working to eradicate poverty in rural communities, and then in southern India doing fundraising and organizational and business development.[1]

"What is AJWS?" we asked.

AJWS was started, the Kleins told us, by Americans who responded as Jews to crises in developing countries by providing humanitarian support. AJWS was distinctive because it sent aid to community-based, grassroots organizations in each area being served, empowering them to effect locally led redevelopment. Ruth W. Messinger became the organization's new president and chief executive officer in 1998, beginning her tenure by providing emergency assistance to victims of Hurricane Mitch across Central America and by building local aid efforts there.[2]

Being a New Yorker, I knew of Ruth W. Messinger. In 1997, she was the first Jewish woman ever, a Democrat, to run for mayor of New York

City, after having been Manhattan Borough president since 1989 and an ally of the first Black mayor David Dinkins (1990–4). Unbeknownst to me, following her mayoral run, she had become CEO of AJWS.

I had the good fortune to interview Ruth W. Messinger at the Utopia Diner in Manhattan in October 2016.[3] Her successful eighteen years at AJWS were just about to end. Over several cups of coffee, she was generous and gracious enough to share details about the Jewish influences on her life and how her position as head of AJWS allowed her to express with a public Jewish voice her organization's commitment to empowering marginalized populations around the globe. It was a position that filled her with pride and satisfaction.

But at the time she ran for mayor of New York City, I was unfortunately not familiar with her deep background in what she calls "social justice Judaism" and how that background shaped her political career.[4] I was coordinating a Jewish Studies Program at Nassau Community College in Garden City, New York. In our classes, we spent some time discussing the mayoral election and Messinger's candidacy. She advocated for small business, job creation, educational reform, trade unions, and gay rights in her bid to unseat the incumbent Rudy Giuliani. Though victory over Giuliani was considered a long shot in 1997, Messinger, who had won the Democratic primary over Al Sharpton, was so enthusiastically supported by Bill Clinton, Ted Kennedy, and Al Gore, among other Democratic leaders, that her win didn't seem impossible.[5] However, Giuliani's law-and-order, pro-big business platform was popular, even with a large segment of the Jewish vote.

We wondered what the particular issues were, if any, that drew Jewish voters to Giuliani. We knew the Jewish population of voters in the citywide primary electorate had dwindled in New York since the 1950s, perhaps due to middle-class Jewish flight from the inner city, and that research of the early 1990s showed that only 20 percent of Jews viewed a candidate's position on Israel as a decisive factor in their vote.[6] Yet, since Messinger's position on Israel illustrated to our Jewish Studies classes the difference between universalism and particularism, we pursued the contrast between the two candidates.[7]

Giuliani represented a particularist view of the Israeli/Palestinian conflict. He viewed Yasser Arafat, the chairman of the Palestinian

Liberation Organization, as a terrorist, despite Arafat's role in the Oslo Peace Accords. Distrusting terrorists, Giuliani upheld the position that there should be no compromise over land between Jews and Palestinians. Messinger, on the other hand, took a universalistic approach toward finding peace, which meant a process that engaged both sides in dialogue. She supported Israeli President Yitzhak Rabin's engagement of Arafat in peace talks. When Messinger was present at the funeral of Yitzhak Rabin in 1995, she said of him, "He's done more to show the world how to create peace than anyone in my lifetime."[8]

Being a progressive feminist Jew and a Democrat, I was sad that Messinger lost the election in 1997. I didn't know what had happened to her when she left New York City politics. She had been on the New York City Council from 1978 to 1989 and was Manhattan Borough President until 1997. But in her political career, Messinger had not explicitly put forward that her platform and policies were informed by and rooted in her longstanding study and practice of universalist Jewish values. I only came to learn the details of her Jewish background in the course of doing research for this book. I learned that because she had a strong sense of Jewish values, becoming CEO of AJWS finally enabled her to present herself publicly as a Jewish change agent in the world.

Now I was following the path of AJWS and was impressed by the new energy and commitment Messinger infused into the organization and thereby expanded its mission. Under Messinger's stewardship, the all-embracing ethical values inherent in Judaism led the organization to become the first and only Jewish organization devoted solely to ending poverty and promoting human rights in the developing world. AJWS would make it known in places from El Salvador to Zimbabwe to Southeast Asia that *tikkun olam* (the repair of the world) is what American Jews are called upon to do in all areas of the globe where help is needed most.[9]

I wanted to understand the origins of Messinger's commitment to the Jewish values behind her public service. Understandably, she had not stressed her Jewish identity in the mayoral election, but I was to learn that even in her early careers in social work, education, and community organizing, as well as in politics, she was following Jewish teachings transmitted by her family, by the Jewish Theological Seminary where her mother served as public relations director for fifty years, and by Rabbi Abraham Joshua Heschel, who was on the seminary faculty.[10] I came to see that what set Messinger apart from Gerda Lerner and Susana Wald was her early internalization, and her later professional externalization, of social justice Judaism.

As European-born Holocaust survivors, Lerner and Wald often felt safer keeping their Jewish identities in the background, as shadow-selves. Fascist propaganda had redefined Judaism during the Holocaust in order to humiliate Jews as inferior human beings. As children and adolescents, Lerner and Wald witnessed how such malign treatment caused Jews constantly to feel vulnerable to ridicule and attack. But Messinger was born into a democratic society and raised in an era of Civil Rights and people's movements. From family, schooling, and universalist Jewish values, she learned of people's entitlement to human rights. When those rights were denied, she learned that struggles in the United States toward social justice could change conditions for the better for the victimized. As CEO of AJWS, she became a model feminist Jewish activist whose work in the world could potentially change the face of what being Jewish means.

Over the years, changing the face of Judaism worldwide meant developing the profile of AJWS to include impressive, ongoing international grant-making to grassroots organizations in marginalized communities; advocacy for human rights policies and legislation in Washington, D.C., domestically and abroad, and supporting various volunteer service programs in developing countries where hundreds of AJWS activists assisted local development efforts.

One of AJWS' longstanding volunteers, Ann Haendel, served in the AJWS Volunteer Corps in parts of Africa and Asia from 1999 until 2012.[11] I had the additional good fortune to befriend Haendel in 2019 and learned about her relationships with co-workers in the kind of detail I did not find in books. I realized that while AJWS' grants changed many people's lives on the macro level by fighting large-scale hunger, poverty, and disease and by strengthening human rights, the micro level of volunteers' work relating day-to-day to co-workers in local, grassroots organizations yielded relationships that became profoundly transformative for all.

Critical Influences

Ruth W. Messinger was born in New York City ten years after Gerda Lerner was born in Vienna, and three years after Susana Wald was born in Budapest. Messinger was raised in a middle-class neighborhood on the Upper West Side of Manhattan. She is six years my senior. Her parents felt strongly about remaining in the multi-racial, multi-ethnic inner city even when friends took flight to Westchester because of changes in the population.[12]

Though Messinger's parents were assimilated Jews who had not been victimized by the Holocaust in Europe, they were deeply involved in the political world around them and lived with full consciousness they had been spared from the great tragedy. Ruth's great-grandparents had settled in New York City in the nineteenth century from Poland and Germany. Ruth's maternal grandparents served for years on boards of Jewish agencies acting on the idea that this is what Jews do to help the other.[13]

Ruth's parents, the Wylers, Wilfred and Marjorie, identified as liberal Democrats and encouraged Ruth's activism around national and international issues by their own example. They believed it was a fundamental Jewish value to use their own good fortune in the service of others and imbued Ruth and her younger sister with that principle. Ruth's father served on the board of the Hebrew Home and Hospital for fifty-five years. Ruth's mother was chair of the Jewish Childcare Association of New York. Giving back meant service to the larger community as well.[14]

To the Wylers, Jewish particularity existed to teach about universality. That is, being Jewish meant caring about the world. Mrs. Wyler's workplace reinforced that concept. As public relations director at Jewish Theological Seminary (JTS), the primary educational and religious center of Conservative Judaism, Marjorie G. Wyler had the privilege of working closely with Rabbi Abraham Joshua Heschel. Heschel joined the faculty when JTS was expanding its programming to bring the ethical, universalistic dimensions of Judaism to the wider society. As a theologian, philosopher, and human rights activist who linked Jewish mysticism with social action, Heschel educated young people to become Jewish community leaders.[15]

Marjorie Wyler was witness to Rabbi Heschel's defining the concept of "social justice Judaism" for the Jewish community. He was a "presence" validating the principle that thinking about the world, and all the people who were in need of help, was a very Jewish thing to do. Ruth's mother's work, much of which she brought home, augmented and intensified Ruth's Jewish education. Mrs. Wyler asked Ruth to assist her at home when she proofread copy from JTS. This practice of learning by reading with her mother taught Ruth a great deal about language and Judaism. She was told that teachers like Rabbi Heschel were important role models and that it was Jewish to apply one's learning out there in the world, especially to meet the needs of the other, today's stranger.[16] Later, as CEO of AJWS, Ruth wrote about the Jewish sources of this ethical imperative.[17] Her drive to meet the needs of "the other" began in her home and in her understanding as a girl to "use her Judaism as a lens for learning about moral courage and obligation."[18] In short, Messinger was raised to connect her Jewish background with social responsibility.

Early Activism: 1950s–60s

Marjorie Wyler encouraged her daughter, Ruth, to learn about political realities as an early teen. Ruth's teenage years were coexistent with the right-wing red scare permeating U.S. politics during the McCarthy Era following World War II. The red-baiting continued with the punitive investigations of liberals by the House Un-American Activities Committee (HUAC), and the controversial execution of the Rosenbergs, two Jews convicted of being spies.[19]

Mrs. Wyler had Ruth stay home from school when she was thirteen to watch part of the nationally televised Army-McCarthy hearings. They resulted in a downturn of public support for Senator Joseph McCarthy, who was systematically targeting liberals as traitors on the basis of insufficient evidence. But the government's attempt to rout out Communists continued with testimonies required of American liberals and progressives by the HUAC.

At age fifteen, Ruth saw the pacifist folk singer and activist Pete Seeger on the very morning of the day he was called to testify before HUAC. Seeger performed regularly at a University Settlement House camp where Ruth worked. HUAC was bent on intimidating and destroying liberals and progressives, especially those like Seeger who were influential because they were in the limelight. Messinger sees these experiences, and the Anti-Vietnam War and Civil Rights Movements she joined in New York two years later, as formative of her lifelong activism for "stopping the spread of war" and for "standing with those who are persecuted because of their beliefs or identity."[20] These causes emboldened her to demonstrate and speak out on behalf of others. She had not yet had any personal encounter with anti-Semitism. Yet the mass movements of the '60s that Messinger joined with thousands of others to protest the actions of the government resonated with the Jewish values that were part of her upbringing.

Later in her life, after being at the helm of AJWS for eighteen years, Messinger's experience "standing with those who are persecuted" took on a moral depth she connected with the Jewish values that had been guiding her work all along. In 2015, reflecting back on her experience, Messinger wrote that when she made herself vulnerable publicly alongside others who were targeted by discrimination, she was, in a sense, fulfilling her personal interpretation of what it meant to be a Jew who was part of the chosen people.[21] Later I discuss how Messinger's reinterpretation of the controversial "chosen people" concept reflects her serious rethinking of its relevance to social justice Judaism without implying Jewish superiority. She gave new meaning to a concept some branches of Judaism have chosen to reject.[22]

Just a few years before Messinger watched the Army-McCarthy hearings on television with her mother, Gerda Lerner was in Hollywood with her husband, Carl, and their children. Carl, a film writer and filmmaker, was being blacklisted for his union activity. To find work, he needed to relocate to New York. At the time, Lerner was not the kind of mother to teach her children about injustice and discrimination by using blacklisting as an example, the way Marjorie Wyler taught Ruth. Lerner did not encourage her children then with lessons about people's rights. The ghosts of 1930s Vienna inhabited Lerner's "underground mentality" and drove her to conceal the blacklist from her children, thinking she would only be burdening them. Instead, she turned inward to private prayer, asking God—a God, incidentally, in whom she didn't believe—to sustain her strength to "save these children from troubled waters."[23]

Having witnessed people being persecuted for what they believed, Messinger got engaged in U.S. political movements by the 1960s

because the ethos of the time and the power of '60s activists spoke
to her values. On the other hand, Susana Wald in Chile began to
withdraw politically at this time. As with Lerner, the ghosts of the
Holocaust past deterred her from engaging politically. Wald had
become a public Surrealist artist and political provocateur in Santiago
when U.S. Cold War politics escalated political conflict in the controversial election of President Salvador Allende. Wald and her family
were caught in the crossfire between the Communist supporters of
President Salvador Allende and Allende's opponents, who were backed
by President Richard Nixon, the C.I.A., and U.S. corporate interests. Wald's Holocaust ghosts were the Stalin-backed Communists
controlling post-war Budapest, the ones who starved her family, and
the Nazis before them who would have deported her if not for Wallenberg and her conversion to Catholicism. When the U.S.-backed,
right-wing military coup to depose Allende was imminent, Wald and
her husband Ludwig fled with their children to Toronto, desperate to
shield their family from harm, and Wald moved away from political
directions of Surrealism toward feminist spirituality to protect her
fragile Jewish core.[24]

Messinger first encountered anti-Semitism in 1963 in the small
rural Oklahoma town devoid of Jews where she and her first husband,
Eli Messinger, moved and held their first jobs. Messinger had been
raised in a family thoroughly comfortable in their identities as Conservative Jews, in a city that, except for Tel Aviv, had the largest Jewish
population of any world city. Messinger felt fortunate to have enjoyed
a setting in which she was unacquainted with personal attacks against
her as a Jew.

But in her new home, she learned of *lawful* restrictions against Jews
and Negroes from acquaintances who had been raised in racist and
anti-Semitic environments. Surrounded by non-Jews, Messinger could
affirm her Jewish identity and gain some comfort in a strange place by
occasionally attending services in a synagogue, especially on the Jewish
High Holidays, even though the synagogue was thirty-five miles away.
The anti-Semitism she experienced caused her to give more thought
to being explicit about who she was, asking herself, "What do I think
about Judaism, how important is it to me, and how do I respond to the

anti-Semitic remarks that are part of people's casual conversation?" She was "suddenly taken with the internal force" of her Judaism.[25]

Messinger perceived her experiences in Oklahoma as transformative in that they sent her in the direction her future would take. She eventually became a change agent in various careers—community organizing, public service, and politics. The seeds of all these careers were planted in a state where she was an outsider, a New Yorker, a woman, and a Jew. She worked in communities unlike the liberal and diverse neighborhoods of her upbringing, communities that were more rural where people were more attached to the status quo, and she could expect resistance to her views. Even so, she seemed to be guided by Jewish ethics she had internalized, principles she would later articulate in two related articles, "Am I My Brother's Keeper if My Brother Lives Halfway Around the World?" and "Am I My Sibling's Keeper if My Sibling Lives Halfway Around the World?"—both about the values underpinning and guiding her leadership of AJWS, values that justified the expansion of the Jewish universe of obligation beyond the Jewish community alone.[26] These articles began with discussion of two basic principles from *Pirkei Avot* (The Ethics of the Fathers), a Talmudic work of rabbinic maxims.

One principle is that the Torah and Jewish law have been passed down from generation to generation so that they may be applied timelessly and with flexibility in order that they be fitting of changing circumstances and changing needs. *Pirkei Avot* 1:1 states: "Moses received the Torah from Sinai and transmitted it to Joshua; Joshua to the elders; the elders to the prophets; and the prophets handed it down to the men of the Great Assembly." Messinger reads these lines by referencing the Sanhedrin rabbis, the rabbis of the supreme Jewish court, who cite God's words in Leviticus 18:5, "You shall keep My laws and My rules, by the pursuit of which man shall live." The Sanhedrin interprets these words to mean: "You should live" by the laws and "not die by them." Messinger concludes that Jewish laws "are living ones"; that is, they are "meant to be adapted and renewed."[27]

Messinger's reading of the nature of Jewish law is characteristic of a universalist approach. A particularist approach is narrower and more literal. Messinger argues in "Am I My Brother's Keeper if My Brother Lives Halfway Around the World?" that as a "living" law, Jewish law can be meant to obligate Jews beyond the Jewish community alone. A living law would obligate Jews to apply the values that the law commands, the values of empathy, generosity, responsibility, and justice, to all peoples. Messinger recognizes that there are particularist "voices" in Jewish tradition that "construct the universe of obligation narrowly, in ways that prioritize the needs of Jews—serving the Jewish poor, providing aid and succor to Israel, supporting Jewish education." Other Jewish voices "cast the net more widely" but only "as a way of building up a reservoir of good will in order . . . to protect and defend Jewish interests." Messinger's universe of Jewish obligation is broader by prioritizing Jewish obligation only in terms of need "regardless of the ethnic, religious, or national identification of the beneficiaries."[28]

The second principle Messinger discusses from *Pirkei Avot* 2:21 relates to the repair of the world; it is a principle Messinger followed time and again in her professional life, even early on in Oklahoma. "It is not necessary to complete the work, but neither are you free to desist from it."[29] One should not be stopped from doing good works because one feels powerless to repair the world completely. Messinger may have felt that the jobs confronting her in Oklahoma were complex and daunting, but she felt responsible for addressing them even if she was unsure of the outcomes.

Messinger engaged, for example, in political organizing for Lyndon Johnson's presidential campaign in a Republican district of Oklahoma, only to find surprisingly that her efforts did contribute to Democratic victories. As a graduate of Radcliffe and with a master's in social work from the University of Oklahoma, Messinger was hired by Oklahoma's Child Welfare Department to run branches in two counties where they needed an MSW in charge to get federal reimbursement. However, the county judge, sheriff, and attorney were resistant to the changes Messinger recommended. But she persisted, knowing the laws were on her side, and access to federal funding was her "weapon." She used the system to enact change despite local biases against her reforms.

In one case, she needed to find foster families for orphaned and homeless children who were being maltreated in group homes. Acting optimistically on the assumption of finding common ground with people of Christian faith even as a Jew, she turned to the local Evangelical communities. When the pastors told their parishioners they could be doing God's work in providing needy children with homes, parishioners did come forward to volunteer. For Messinger, the skills she gained in Oklahoma working within systems resistant to change would serve her well in her later government and human rights work—how to manage an organization, how to find common ground with people of strongly different backgrounds, and how to change long-standing status quos.[30]

Interestingly, the skills that Messinger learned in Oklahoma she encouraged in AJWS volunteers serving around the globe forty years later, skills that served to empower the volunteers utilizing them as well as the communities benefitting from them.

Non-Racist Education and Social Justice Judaism

When Messinger returned to New York in 1965, she found that her Oklahoma experiences had prepared her to negotiate with New York City government at a time of ferment over people's movements and community insistence on greater control over their neighborhoods and schools. Her good diplomacy skills were at a premium. They enabled her to find people willing to make common cause over issues that characterized several breakdowns of Jewish/Black relations during this period, breakdowns that haven't yet been resolved.[31]

Messinger had become an advocate for non-racist schools, child welfare, and human service programs. After becoming a case worker in the South Bronx and an activist in the Anti-Vietnam War and anti-nuclear proliferation movements, she joined parents on the west side of Manhattan to establish The Children's Community Workshop School. She now resided on the Upper West Side, her old neighborhood, with her husband and their three children. Her children attended this new innovative school, which became a model for economic and racial diversity in education. Launching it, Messinger worked with parents from a full range of backgrounds to advocate for support from city government.[32]

At a time when public education in New York City was fraught with racial tension over demands for decentralization or community control of schools, The Children's Community Workshop School was a successful model, like a "charter school before its time," according to *Times* reporter Frank Bruni, where parents of diverse backgrounds economically, racially and culturally were having "more say in their children's education." Messinger was assistant to the director of the school and "helped forge its vision of more open classrooms and more innovative teaching methods." Most importantly, "she raised money to keep the school afloat while lobbying city officials to adopt it into the public system."[33]

Because Messinger's advocacy skills were obvious, she was urged by the parents of The Community Workshop School to run for the school board. She won a seat on the board and served from 1975–77, during which time she was appointed to be liaison to legislators and often fought with New York City's Board of Education on behalf of the less fortunate in the city. As Messinger herself states in a booklet celebrating her career, *Messinger of Hope*, "We disagreed with the Central Board of Education, and we fought them on many different occasions. I learned a lot about organizing for change."[34]

Surprisingly, the way Messinger described what she learned from these early New York experiences sounds like a paraphrase of the *Pirkei Avot* reference in her later writing. "Our school board was making a lot of trouble and I was one of the lead troublemakers. . . . I was . . . demonstrating to people that you can make change. . . . *You don't get everything you started out looking for, but you do get something*."[35] While Messinger knew the task was large, and she didn't fully complete the work, she didn't desist either, and she made significant progress. Even later, when Messinger ran for New York City Council representing the West Side of Manhattan and won the seat she occupied from 1977–89, she sounded again as if *Pirkei Avot* were guiding her. She said she learned "how to challenge the powers that be, put forward significant proposals for change, and recognize that progress comes slowly." In this office, "she became known" for many wonderful projects, including moving "city money to . . . public education programs."[36]

More funding for public education programs was sorely needed, especially in city neighborhoods that were economically and racially segregated by redlining, a process by which banks, realtors, and insurance companies would convince white working-class and middle-class families living in communities throughout the boroughs to sell their homes.

Gerda Lerner lived in a once racially integrated neighborhood in St. Albans, Queens, that had been redlined. Hers was one of only two white families that remained. Lerner's family remained in the neighborhood because, like Messinger, Lerner was determined that her children would attend school and "mix naturally and on a daily basis with children of color so that they would grow up as free from prejudices as possible."[37] The commitment that Lerner and Messinger shared to having their children attend multi-racial schools was rooted in their mutual desire as Jews to have their children learn not to treat people from different races, classes, or cultures as "others," the way Jews historically had been treated.

Messinger reminded me as I was writing this chapter that the failures in the New York City education system went way beyond redlining. While inequity along color lines was worse in poor neighborhoods, it was visible even in integrated neighborhoods, as on the Upper West Side where Messinger lived. Racial integration in classes was often not enforced in public schools because of special programs and tracking, some of that promoted by white parents. The Children's Community Workshop School opposed these behaviors. It was fully integrated and untracked, which Messenger said "did not make it an island of perfection but at least a real place."[38] Race combined with economic class discrimination is not easily or quickly overcome. Yet federal law required public schools to desegregate despite income disparities between the segregated, geographically distant Black and white neighborhoods where busing was tried, unsuccessfully.

In New York City, using busing to integrate public schools was opposed by "hordes of white mothers" who protested for "neighborhood schools," claiming busing caused too many "hardships" for their children and broke their ties with their neighborhoods, according to journalist Rebecca Klein. Their rhetoric camouflaged racist attitudes— that is, their unwillingness to have their children attend school and mix with Black and Puerto Rican students and their fear that those students of color would be bused into their neighborhoods. That these attitudes were growing among conservative Jewish urbanites in northern cities has been researched by American Jewish historian Murray I. Friedman.[39] Black students may have also experienced busing as difficult, since supports for their adjustments to white schools were often not provided, as one anecdotal report about Midwood High School in Brooklyn revealed.[40]

Yet Messinger learned a different story from a white married couple who had derived benefits from attending the well-known Little Rock Central High School in Arkansas in the late 1950s when Black students were bused in under protection from the U.S. Army. Messinger spoke to the couple when she was a graduate student in social work in Oklahoma. The couple had not been kept home by their parents, as many white students had been. The couple's parents "were determined to see their own kids advance." Racist attitudes had not blocked them. They kept their children in school while it was being integrated. From the married couple, Messinger learned that their experiences in the racially mixed school actually inspired them to "study social work and to adopt a much more progressive stance on issues of race and education." Because Messinger was moved by this couple's experience, their story was included in AJWS' booklet *Messinger of Hope.*[41]

The hoped-for solution of creating integrated schools makes all the more heartbreaking the devastation in the New York City public school system that occurred in the 1960s after experiments in busing failed. The city's subsequent attempt to decentralize schools with community control resulted in a breakdown between the newly appointed Black leadership in one new district, Ocean Hill-Brownsville, and the teachers' union, The United Federation of Teachers (UFT). The three massive city-wide strikes—called by UFT President Albert Shanker after nine teachers, mostly Jewish, were transferred out of Ocean Hill-Brownsville in 1968— accelerated the Black/Jewish divide that had been brewing.[42]

During this period of ferment over civil rights, Messinger—who had recently returned to New York City from Oklahoma—was devoted to bringing people and communities together across lines of difference, even before her career in New York City politics began. She was influenced by her mother who joined Rabbi Abraham Joshua Heschel on the Civil Rights March from Selma to Montgomery in 1965. Heschel "marched arm-in-arm with Martin Luther King, Jr." on that day and "likened civil rights activism to 'praying with my feet.'" In 1968, Messinger participated in the Poor People's Campaign for economic justice on the National Mall in Washington, D.C., with her children in tow. She had been working with an organization committed to fighting racism in schools and in the criminal justice system and to creating greater racial and economic equity by providing affordable housing.[43]

The Jewish leadership creating alliances with the Civil Rights Movement for Blacks emphasized two main narratives in Jewish texts that also underlie Messinger's calling. Messinger pointed me, during my interview with her in 2016, to the important speech delivered by Conservative Rabbi Joachim Prinz, who joined Reverend Martin Luther King, Jr. on the 1963 March on Washington for Jobs and Freedom. Rabbi Prinz represented the World Jewish Congress. In his speech on which the documentary *I Shall Not Be Silent* is based, he stressed the important lesson coming out of his experience as a refugee from Hitler that Jews are obligated not to stand idly by in the face of any and all forms of discrimination. Moreover, he emphasized that the command to Jews to love their neighbor was a moral command, not a matter of geography.

> In the realm of the spirit, our fathers taught us thousands of years ago that when God created man, he created him as everybody's neighbor. Neighbor is not a geographical term. It is a moral concept. It means our collective responsibility for the preservation of man's dignity and integrity.[44]

A theme running through this book is that Jewish "difference" can only flourish civilly and properly when an overarching universalism simultaneously fosters Jewish appreciation and respect for the cultural and faith traditions of others. As a Jew, Rabbi Prinz saw the fight against Nazism and the fight against racial injustice as morally the same. This was the kind of universalism Messinger also found in Rabbi Heschel's teachings, and she brought her understanding of universalism into her leadership of AJWS as a social justice Jew obligated to eradicating injustice globally.

The Concept of the Chosen People

Messinger encountered a political challenge in the 1980s when she served on the New York City Council and was fighting for gay rights. Messinger wrote to me that "there was a lot at stake" with this cause and she "did what" she "had to do." In her article "Bridging the Near and Far," written during the heart of the AIDS crisis, Messinger wrote that "time and again, I was heartbroken as friends and constituents lost their lives to a deadly disease and suffered the effects of ignorance, fear, and hate."[45]

The implications of that struggle evidently reverberated for many years in Messinger's thoughts, because nine years later she wrote vividly about that day in 1986 when, on the floor of the City Council, she defended New York City's first bill to protect the rights of gays and lesbians. In her article she developed a unique and penetrating interpretation of what it means for her as a Jew to be part of the "chosen people," a concept she maintains in a personal and original way.[46]

I wish to make clear that my understanding of Messinger's Jewish universalism reflects my own conclusions about her beliefs, how they fit together, and how they compare with traditional ideas. My interpretations are speculations and suggestions that should not be read as Messinger's own articulations.

Traditional Jewish interpretations of the "chosen people" cite the covenant given by God to Moses at Sinai as a contract that promises the Jewish people God's blessing and their continuity as long as they follow God's commandments. In this way of reading the events at Sinai, Jews have been "chosen" by God to enter into a specific and close relationship. In a manual AJWS provided its volunteers so they would have a basic Judaism to fall back on, *chosenness* is explained as "the particular covenantal relationship to God" that the Jews chose, and "God chose this particular relationship with the Jews."[47]

The concept is controversial in that some branches of Judaism carry chosenness further to mean that Jews have an historic and divinely mandated mission on behalf of all Jewry to relay the truth of God's message to the world, since they compose "a nation of individuals who have been given the opportunity to sense G—d's closeness."[48] Other branches of Judaism relate to the "chosen people" differently. Classic Reconstructionism, for example, has eliminated the concept entirely from their mode of worship.[49] Other branches emphasize Jews as the "choosing" people, people who have been given the opportunity to choose to follow God's commandments.[50]

Messinger developed yet another interpretation of the "chosen people" when in 2015 she wrote "Bridging the Near and Far" for *Sh'ma Journal*. She was reflecting back on the AIDS crisis and the time she was advancing New York City's first anti-discrimination bill to protect the rights of gays and lesbians in housing, employment, and public accommodation, all areas where gays were being subjected to discrimination, harassment, and disparate treatment. Messinger was up against a mighty, opposing coalition among the Roman Catholic Church, some Orthodox Jewish groups, and conservative religious leaders. By 1986 she was the City Council floor manager defending the bill, and "the hearing was not progressing well." She thought of young police officer Charlie Cochran who had made a huge impact on her and others because of the risk he took speaking out.[51]

Messinger remembered how sometime before the hearing, Cochran had made himself vulnerable to stigma and announced publicly that he himself was gay. Remembering his testimony "coming out" publicly to support the bill emboldened Messinger to bring the vote to pass. This experience of remembering Cochran's brave example led Messinger masterfully to connect the concept of chosenness in her article for *Sh'ma* to the call for Jews publicly to stand up and risk being discredited themselves when extending compassion to others who suffer from bias and discrimination. [52]

By 2015, after many years' experience being a public Jew in her AJWS work, Messinger realized that what Charlie Cochran did by making himself vulnerable to stigma was a model for how Jews, like herself, are obligated to respond in solidarity when others are suffering from discrimination. "Embracing Chosenness," she wrote, "means accepting a moral mandate to speak for and with those whose dignity has been denied." Jews have to come out publicly when others are treated unfairly despite the taint we may invoke upon ourselves. Being Jewish means choosing to root "our lives in ethical obligations." It means "figuring out how to negotiate the dynamics of being different and advocating for those who are perceived as different . . . especially when the act of doing so renders us vulnerable too."[53]

Messinger's understanding of chosenness reflects her closeness to the teachings of Rabbi Heschel whose writings and ideas permeated her household during her formative years. In a 1973 interview shortly before Heschel died, he summarized his major moral teachings about God's intentions for granting freedom and choice to human beings. According to Heschel, God's hope is that freedom and choice lead humans to learn about ethical obligations, and that "a life without discipline was not worth living."[54] What is unique in Judaism to Heschel is not Jewish moral superiority but rather the view of "man's tremendous potentiality" to be God's ethical partner.[55] God is searching for man. God is waiting for man, to whom God gave freedom, to choose partnership in bringing about a time of compassion and justice.

Heschel's concept of a human partnership with God leads him to explore God's need for man as much as man's need for God. As God's partner, man is meant to remind God of himself. Man reminds God of the need for compassion and justice. "Do I have to tell you," Heschel asked his interviewer, "[that] the greatness of man is that he faces problems. I would judge a person by how many deep problems he's concerned with." The relationship between man and God thus becomes reflexive; they become models for one another. "As God is compassionate, let man be compassionate. As God strives for meaning and justice, let man strive for meaning and justice." Heschel said the prophets are able to show us how to hold God and man together in this way "in one thought." The prophets help us understand that "what I do to man, I do to God. When I hurt a human being, I injure God."[56]

To the idea of one nation singled out for an automatic special relationship to God, Heschel responded in the following way:

> I think God loves all men. He has given many nations. He has given all men an awareness of His greatness and His love. And God is to be found in many hearts all over world. Not limited to one nation or to one people, to one religion. . . . God is either the Father of all man or of no man.[57]

To the interviewer's question, "Would it be a better world if we were all of one religion?" Heschel responded, "No . . . I think it is the will of God that there should be religious pluralism."[58]

Like Heschel, Messinger rejects any exaltation of Jewish people implied by the "chosen people" concept without completely abandoning the concept. Whereas Heschel stresses the Jewish belief that humans have the potential to choose partnership with God, Messinger stresses the opportunity Jews have to choose partnership with other individuals and groups persecuted for being different. Identifying with others who are tagged for being different because of who they are creates bonds serving the dignity of all human beings and the eradication of injustice.

In this view, chosenness comes close to other Jewish precepts integrated into AJWS manuals on Judaism given to staff, volunteers, and in-country representatives for reference during periods of service. These precepts include loving the stranger, the outsider, as oneself, and viewing all human beings as created in the image of God (*b'tzelem elohim*).[59]

The reader may recall that Susana Wald linked persecution, difference, and choice in much the same way that Messinger explains chosenness. Wald, who felt like an "outsider" wherever she sought refuge from persecution as a Holocaust survivor, chose to adopt "cover" identities to mute and protect her fragile Jewish core. But she finally felt compelled to "come out" publicly as a Jew during the Insurrection in Oaxaca, in a thoroughly anti-Semitic environment, in order to speak out and align herself with the people's movement for social and economic justice.[60] Wald chose the kind of full self-disclosure and vulnerability that Messinger respected and admired in Charlie Cochran.

On the other hand, Gerda Lerner understood the "chosen people" concept more traditionally to mean the elevation of the Jewish people, specifically the males, separate and apart from other peoples of the world. For Lerner this meaning of chosenness is fraught with contradictions in the context of Judaism's universal values. By age fourteen in 1934 Vienna, Lerner had become disillusioned with her Orthodox congregation's unequal treatment of the poor, the working classes, and women. By the time she wrote as an accomplished scholar about Genesis, God's blessing of the unified Hebrew tribes under the leadership of Abram, and the special mark of Jewish bonding to God represented by male circumcision, she was already critiquing the historical contributions of Judaism to the dominance of patriarchy in *The Creation of Patriarchy*.[61] For her, the "chosen people" concept first introduced in Genesis was another example of male inclusivity alone.

As for myself, the traditional view of the "chosen people" concept struck a dissonant chord as a departure from the more democratic and leveling impulses of Judaism, the compassion for the stranger, the caring for widows and orphans, the relinquishment of all debts in the sabbatical year. As a college literature student and young adult teacher of English, I was influenced by psychological and anthropological perspectives and began to view the chosen people as a compensatory myth, not unlike the Christian concept of "the last shall be first."

In contrast, the meaning Messinger seems to give to the chosen people is a reworking of the call in the prophet Isaiah 42:6 for Jews to be "a light of nations" by their acts of loving kindness (*gemilut Hasidim*) and their repair of the world (*tikkun olam*). Instead, Messinger seems to call on Jews to be lights *among* the nations, encouraging Jews to choose upholding the dignity of all those in need who are unjustly marginalized. A donor to AJWS, Rabbi Steven Leder came to the same conclusion about AJWS after organizing a Study Tour on poverty to Uganda: "You can't be a light unto the nations if you're not among the nations. What I love about AJWS is that it's among the nations, doing this work within a Jewish context."[62]

Through AJWS, Messinger envisioned Jews acting on universalist values throughout the world—not only on the macro level with many levels of service internationally, but also on the micro level with the Volunteer Corps, an integral part of AJWS until 2013.

Expanding the Jewish Universe of Obligation on the Macro Level

Expanding the ways AJWS applied Jewish values to the repair of the world in the areas where it is needed most is Messinger's hallmark and signature achievement. It is the accomplishment that earned her recognition as "La Pasionara of Jewish social activism" according to the *Jewish Daily Forward*, which included her in its "Forward 50" list of influential Jews for nearly a decade beginning in 2005.[63] The *Jerusalem Post* considered her the sixth most influential Jew in the world.[64] In 2006, the *Jewish Daily Forward* hailed her many accomplishments, which have grown significantly since then: "No single American has been more central in mobilizing public protest over the genocide in Sudan; it's part of her larger vision of religious engagement with Africa and the Third World."[65] By 2016, when Messinger retired from the presidency of AJWS to become its first Global Ambassador, AJWS published a tribute biography of her that acknowledged her remarkable contributions to the organization:

> Under her leadership, AJWS has granted more than $300 million to more than 1,000 grassroots organizations in dozens of developing countries and has launched campaigns to end the Darfur genocide, reform international food aid, stop violence against women, respond to natural disasters worldwide and defend land rights for indigenous farmers.[66]

In reflecting on her eighteen-year leadership of AJWS, Messinger herself attributed her universalist outlook on activism to Rabbi Heschel. She referred to Heschel's often-quoted concept about responsibility: "In a free society, where terrible wrongs exist, some are guilty but all are responsible." Messinger said this "ethic" of Heschel's "motivated the work I did in the 60s, and . . . motivates me in AJWS today." She continued to say in AJWS' biography of her, "I didn't cause urban racism or bad schools, I didn't cause land theft in Guatemala. But I'm still responsible for it." She goes on to say:

> In some cases, the problems that exist in the world were created by the U.S. government; and in other cases, we are responsible purely because we are human and we are citizens of the world. Either way, as a Jew, I have to act, I have to assume responsibility for things that aren't the way they ought to be, and I have to work to create greater justice.[67]

While the problems of the world Messinger first addressed as AJWS CEO included Hurricane Mitch in Central America, the earthquakes in El Salvador and Turkey, and the "ethnic cleansing" in Kosovo, it was the disasters of 2004–5 that brought worldwide attention to the organization. Messinger's immediate reactions to the tsunami that struck the coast of southeast Asia and the genocide that was plaguing Black Africans in the Darfur region of Sudan galvanized support that "nearly doubled AJWS' budget and enabled it to launch massive responses to both crises."[68]

In southeast Asia, AJWS' response was distinctive in that it provided not only relief for victims of the tsunami, as did other international aid groups, but it also worked alongside local grantees over several years doing development building in five countries as well as human rights work. Messinger said, "When AJWS responds to disasters, we stay for the long haul so people can recover, change their circumstances and realize their rights."[69]

To respond to the horrors happening in Darfur, Messinger directed AJWS to mobilize the Jewish community and other U.S. faith-based groups. As soon as the confluence of mass slaughter, rapes, burnings, shellings, and bombings of Black African villages by government enlisted Arab Janjaweed militias was declared a genocide by Congress and the White House, Messinger convened a multi-organizational meeting, enlisting Elie Wiesel to speak. Jews and non-Jews subsequently founded the Save the Darfur Coalition.[70]

During the time of the genocide, AJWS was able to fund grantees in Darfur and Chad with over five million dollars to save lives and end atrocities. Jews around the U.S. were choosing AJWS as their vehicle to respond as Messinger reminded them in spirited talks of Jewish history, the Holocaust, and the obligation Jews have to act on the promise of "Never Again!" by not standing idly by when genocide is raging.[71] In 2008, after having visited refugee camps in Sudan and Chad, Messinger addressed a Darfur benefit:

> As Jews, our own deep pain—from 70 years ago—reminds us what is lost when people and nations remain bystanders to genocide. This is why AJWS has spent six years organizing a community of activists that now numbers 70,000 strong. This is why we have provided critical life-saving medical care, critical counseling and essential services to people displaced by the genocide.[72]

In the sister articles Messinger co-authored with Aaron Dorfman ("Am I My Brother's Keeper" and "Am I My Sister's Keeper"), Messinger and Dorfman cite the great medieval rabbi and scholar Maimonides extensively for justifying the expansion of the Jewish obligation to promote economic justice beyond the Jewish community alone.[73] By referencing Hannah Arendt's criticism of "pity" toward people in unfortunate circumstances in *On Revolution* ("pity . . . can be enjoyed for its own sake"),[74] Messinger and Dorfman close their articles explaining why as

Jews we must move beyond "pity" in response to poverty, suffering, and disease in the developing world. I choose to use the word *charity* as Messinger and Dorfman used *pity*. We must move beyond pity and charity because in both cases, these responses serve mainly to make *us* feel "good." And if pity makes us feel good, according to Messinger and Dorfman, "we're inclined to perpetuate the circumstances that engendered the feeling."[75] Messinger and Dorfman then quote Susan Sontag to explain that by feeling good about our sympathy (or our pity or our charity), we relieve our consciences and thus remove ourselves from responsibility for the causes of the suffering.[76] This is not what Messinger and Dorfman believe Jewish tradition teaches us.

The authors cite "the central command of the Passover Seder" which is, as they see it, for us "to see ourselves as if *we* have been freed from slavery." We aren't commanded to pity the slaves, but to find ways of reliving the slave experience, with unleavened bread, bitter herbs, and recitation of the plagues. In other words, to really become aware of the impoverishment of others, we need to connect with their experience of it, not distance ourselves from it.[77] As one definition of *tzedakah*—the Hebrew term for social and economic justice—puts it, "This critical social responsibility cannot be done to someone—rather, it must be done with someone."[78] Messinger and Dorfman make their final point by quoting the Australian Aboriginal activist Lila Watson: "If you have come to help me you are wasting your time. But if you have come here because your liberation is bound up with mine, let us work together."[79]

AJWS' Work Internationally on the Macro Level: The Case of Sex Workers in Thailand

Women's empowerment is a longstanding part of AJWS' mission and its grants portfolio. Funds from the Charles H. Revson Foundation in part made it possible for AJWS to publish a High School and Adult Education Module in 2006, *Women's Empowerment: Global Perspectives*, that shows how "gender cuts across all issues" of concern to AJWS. The module covers the topics of women, poverty, and development; gender-based violence; women in disasters and conflict situations; women and education; gender and health; working with men, and women's empowerment in the Jewish tradition.[80]

The module contains a section on "Sex-work and Trafficking" with examples from Thailand, where AJWS grants have been improving the rights, safety, education, vocational skills, and health of sex workers through organizations like EMPOWER and Asia Pacific Network of Sex Workers.[81] I focus on the issue of sex workers as a case study because it illustrates AWJS' ability to employ Jewish values to inform its response to a controversial and marginalized group of women in need who require being understood on their own terms.

AJWS was already granting funds to the above organizations that safeguard the rights, safety, and educational opportunities of sex workers in Thailand, when Messinger visited the country around 2011, presented a talk about her experience (2013), and then published a written version of it in *Messinger of Hope*.[82] The published article, "Reframing the *Sh'ma* to Repair the World," includes the Hebrew *Sh'ma* meaning "hear" or "listen" and emphasizes how listening is the Jewish key to helping other nations. Traditionally, the *Sh'ma* is associated with the central Jewish prayer *Sh'ma Israel* ("Listen Israel"), God is One. In her article, Messinger focuses on the centrality of listening to the Jewish experience, this time in understanding people about whom we have prejudices and whose circumstances and cultures are different from ours.

A foundational axiom of AJWS is the Jewish value of empowerment as the way to help those in need. According to twelfth-century rabbi and philosopher Maimonides, empowerment is the highest level of the "Eight Levels of *Tzedakah*" outlined in his *Mishneh Torah*, a codification of Jewish law. What other faith traditions identify as charity, Jewish tradition identifies as *tzedakah* ("social and economic justice") from the root word for justice, *tzedek*. The highest level of *tzedakah* is empowerment, helping those in need to gain equal footing with others in order to survive and become self-supporting.[83]

Messinger wrote specifically about empowerment in an early article on how her values as a social worker empowering low-income urban adults influenced her political work on the City Council of New York.[84] However, in this article Messinger does not refer to the Jewish origins of empowerment as an ethical practice. AJWS literature, on the other hand, does connect empowerment with Maimonides' highest level of *tzedakah*.[85]

In Thailand and in other countries around the world, the question arises: How can AJWS empower sex workers if they voluntarily choose sex work? Initially, as a feminist, Messinger thought of sex work only as oppression. Her view was broadened, however, by following the *Sh'ma*, the Jewish imperative to listen. By listening, Messinger gained understanding that brought her beyond the judgment that prostitution—selling sex for money—was "immoral and coercive." From listening to "countless stories from sex workers themselves" in both developed and developing countries, Messinger learned not only how thoroughly sex workers were discriminated against, but also how sex work could be less exploitative than other limited options of work available to women, especially those who were mothers and needed time to care for children.[86]

In Thailand, Messenger spoke to a thirty-seven-year-old sex worker, a mother of three, who had chosen sex work as a way to survive. Messinger learned that this woman's only other option was sweatshop labor: sewing buttons on shirts, ten hours a day, away from her children, for a per diem salary of two dollars. The woman explained:

> "Or, I could spend the day with my kids and, at night, talk to an interesting western man, lie down with him for 20 minutes in a familiar, safe place, and make a lot of money. Which would you choose?"

Messinger concluded about this woman and others like her,

> Who am I to tell them their labor is any less valid than my own? Who am I to believe that this woman is any less deserving of physical safety and the right to earn a living—rights that I fully enjoy and have long taken for granted?[87]

The result for AJWS is a policy that does "not take either a pro- or anti-legalization position on prostitution." Instead AJWS follows its grantees' leads:

> . . . the ones who are and who work with sex workers, as to what advocacy and service provision will result in the best environment

and opportunities for the women. . . . Grantees include organizations which both support and empower sex workers and also ones who strive to provide alternatives to sex work for vulnerable populations.[88]

With this enlightened perspective on the needs of sex workers, AJWS has expanded its grant-giving as of 2019 to thirty-five organizations that ensure the safety and health of sex workers—thirty-five out of 161 organizations that receive AJWS grants promoting sexual health and rights for women, girls, and LGBTQI people.[89]

AJWS' Work Internationally on the Micro Level: The Volunteer Corps

The AJWS volunteers I've read about who served in the Volunteer Corps—skilled professionals who spent three months to a year working with grassroots organizations around the globe to promote sustainable development and human rights—came to connect their own lives in intimate ways with the people with whom they lived and worked. I learned about several Volunteer Corps members from Ann Haendel, who participated in the Volunteer Corps from 1999 until 2012, fulfilling seven different assignments in various countries in Africa and Asia, service atypical in its length and depth. That AJWS provided Haendel with the opportunity to do so many different placements, including excessively challenging ones, was unique. Almost all of AJWS' volunteers in every different program did one program or assignment; just a few did two or three.

Through interviews with Haendel, and the generous access she provided me to many materials in her personal library documenting her experiences, I learned how relationships between herself as an AJWS volunteer and her local, grassroots co-workers could embody the goal of empowerment as an example of social justice Judaism.[90]

In AJWS, in order for the *tzedakah*/empowerment relationship to be completed, the giver—whether an individual or an organization initiating the relationship—also becomes a receiver.[91] This was true for Rabbi Steven Leder who was not a member of the Volunteer Corps, but who organized a shorter Study Tour to Uganda that incorporated volunteer service. He said, "AJWS's work isn't just universal; it's also particular in its impact on Jews":

> Changing the lives of others changes us. The people who traveled with me and AJWS to Uganda were deeply affected in a positive way. It is a very important Jewish value that we treat other people in a way we want to be treated.[92]

I learned how this type of *tzedakah* arrangement unfolded in the longer-term experience of Ann Haendel. In a talk called "The House the Beads Built" that Haendel presented to a Jewish audience in St. Petersburg, Florida, in April 2020, she explained that AJWS had assigned her in late 2001 to work with a local organization in Kampala, Uganda, The National Community of Women Living with AIDS (NACWOLA). Their mission was to educate Ugandans about HIV/AIDS prevention and how to minimize stigma. HIV/AIDS was rampant, and the entire NACWOLA staff was HIV positive; Haendel was not. This contributed to their perception of her as an outsider about whom they had their suspicions. The director under whom Haendel was to work was away in London, and the acting director was not equipped to supervise Haendel's expertise in organizational development, based on her experience in Washington, D.C.

Haendel discovered personal skills in herself that *empowered* her to find ways of adapting to unexpected circumstances. She needed to develop a personal tool kit for emotional survival in a disorienting and not-so-friendly environment. After notifying AJWS of the situation, she was not only granted approval to assist other groups (other NGOS and Makere University), but also was asked to make several site visits to prospective AJWS grantees in Uganda, followed by reports and recommendations.

Haendel's work at NACWOLA became part-time basic report writing. She was unexpectedly befriended by the organization's cook, Yudaya, who was herself struggling with AIDS. By offering Haendel friendship and home hospitality, Yudaya contributed to Haendel's empowerment and her ability to overcome obstacles in her work environment. Their relationship became long-lasting. For her part, Haendel empowered Yudaya in ways that conformed more traditionally to Maimonides' conception of *tzedakah*.

In Haendel's talk, she described Yudaya's living conditions: the overcrowded, bare-bones, brick dwelling in which she lived with her four children and family of cousins. With only an outdoor pit for a kitchen, Yudaya served Haendel a festive meal of chicken, rice, and bananas that must have cost Yudaya a fortune. Ten years later, when Haendel reunited with Yudaya in Uganda on her way to another AJWS assignment in Kenya, Haendel told her audience they "hugged like sisters," and Haendel slept overnight in Yudaya's new dwelling, the house the beads built. Yudaya had been able to build her new home in part because of Haendel's unusual and remarkable assistance that contributed to Yudaya's gaining greater self-sufficiency.

Haendel's approach to her work in 2002 fighting AIDS alongside Yudaya and other staff members reflected AJWS' core philosophy, rooted in Maimonides, to let other people decide their own direction and pursue their own visions of justice toward the goal of self-sufficiency. Haendel explained in her talk that she told her co-workers "to do what *they* wanted to do, not what I *told* them to do." She elaborated with a domestic metaphor. "They set the table, and I just tried to help them strengthen the legs." In the case of Yudaya, Haendel indeed "strengthened the legs" of her "table," metaphorically speaking.

Yudaya had been accumulating "bits and pieces" over many years to build her "dream house," Haendel told us. Yudaya and her four children learned how to fashion colorful paper beads in 2007 by rolling up small strips of recycled magazine paper, shellacking them and stringing them together. That summer, when Haendel was back in her St. Petersburg home, she received a package from Yudaya containing over one thousand colorful necklaces and bracelets with the note: "Please sell." In Haendel's own written piece about this experience, "The Visit," she wrote, "I became a bead merchant."[93] Selling the jewelry at gatherings to friends and family and at a program she arranged on Women in Africa at a local restaurant, Haendel collected over three thousand dollars in less than four years. Sending Yudaya the money via Western Union and Moneygram, Haendel provided the balance Yudaya needed for materials to complete her dream house, the very house Haendel visited in 2012—a house with three bedrooms, a living room, a separate dining room, a small kitchen, and a bathroom. In large measure, Haendel had contributed to Yudaya's journey toward self-sufficiency.

It turned out for Haendel that working within NACWOLA and befriending Yudaya helped them both see more clearly the ways their lives were entwined, the way women across lines of class, race, culture, and religion could view and relate to one another with respect and helpfulness. The words of Australian Aboriginal activist Lila Watson bear repeating here: "If you have come to help me you are wasting your time. But if you have come here because your liberation is bound up with mine, let us work together."[94]

AJWS discontinued the Volunteer Corps in 2013 in order to focus more fully "on U.S. based programs that advocate for global justice."[95] To create global justice, "upstream" work on United States' and others' policy, legislation, and practice is required, more so than "downstream" service programs, such as the Volunteer Corps. The service programs, which had great impact for the volunteers in them, do not carry the same weight in the policy world.[96]

In the 2019 *AJWS Annual Report*, those "upstream" programs included grant-making to advance human rights and end poverty in the developing world, AJWS staff coalitions to advance U.S. legislation and policy-making on Capitol Hill for the same human rights issues supported by the grants, coalitions by rabbis and their congregants across the U.S. to support AJWS staff in Washington, D.C., and emergency aid to respond to crises such as the Rohingya genocide in Burma, among other important causes.[97]

In *I Am Jewish*, a volume of short essays compiled in honor of reporter Daniel Pearl who was brutally murdered in 2002 by Islamic terrorists in Pakistan at the same time that he was affirming his Jewish identity, Messinger's essay in the collection expresses in a nutshell her aspirations for what AJWS might contribute to Jews' understanding of themselves and their calling:

> As a Jew, I am working with grassroots groups in Africa, Asia, Latin America, the Middle East, Russia, and Ukraine, feeding the hungry, caring for the stranger, and defeating the oppressions

that plague so many. And I envision a day when service by Jews, in a Jewish context, will become a rite of passage in and for the Jewish community. It will be done by people of all ages, from teens to seniors, and involve work with Jews and non-Jews. . . .

We will make a dramatic difference in attracting Jews to more active Judaism, changing the ways in which Jews are seen around the world and changing the ways in which Jews understand their global obligations.[98]

American Jewish World Service and Israel

Inasmuch as AJWS promotes expansion of American Jewish obligation around the world, its training manual of 2009 included among the Frequently Asked Questions: What is AJWS' position on the state of Israel? Does AJWS work in Israel? If not, why not? The responses included affirmation of Israel as a democratic state working toward peace in the midst of violence, terrorism, anti-Semitism, and bigotry. AJWS also supported "the right of the Palestinian people to live in dignity and to have their human rights respected" and rejected violence as a means toward achieving peace between Israelis and Palestinians.[99]

AJWS explained further that it does not itself work in Israel for several reasons, a main one being the work many other organizations perform that "support development and human rights in Israel, the West Bank and Gaza." Also, there are many other organizations that "are working to resolve the Israeli-Palestinian conflict." Beyond that, AJWS reiterated its loyalty to its main mission as "the only U.S.-based Jewish organization expressly dedicated to alleviating poverty and supporting human rights in the regions of Latin America, Africa and Asia." AJWS also clarified that since its American Jewish supporters and its grassroots grantees around the globe represent a wide diversity of opinion about the Israeli-Palestinian conflict, AJWS wishes to preserve the coalition of support it already has developed for doing its work in Asia, Africa, and Latin America.[100]

These positions were challenged in 2011 when AJWS participated in a side project at the request of a donor, a trip to Israel in 2012 in partnership with Avodah, another progressive Jewish group whose mission includes promoting social and economic justice. The problem over the itinerary, which omitted any visit to the territories of the West Bank and Gaza and any interactions with Palestinians, was resolved quickly by Messinger, after an Avodah staff member resigned and Avodah staff members launched a petition in opposition to the trip.[101]

Messinger told *The Forward*, "We've heard some concerns, and we're going to take them under consideration."[102] The issues were discussed, and ultimately a compromise itinerary resulted that was acceptable to all sides. Meetings were arranged in Jerusalem proper to discuss challenges faced by Ethiopian Jews and Israeli Arabs. Meetings were also organized with activist groups like Ir Amin regarding East Jerusalem, and the Holy Land Trust regarding nonviolent resistance in Palestine. B'Tselem would lead a tour of Hebron in the West Bank. Participants would meet with the Shalom Hartman Institute and with Shatil, the New Israel Fund's civil society-building program in Israel.[103]

These compromises among AJWS and the other organizations involved offer hope at a time when young Jews in particular find it hard to join American Jewish groups currently practicing the silencing of discussion around the Israeli-Palestinian divide. Instead, by taking the challenge of entering discussion, AJWS and Avodah managed to maintain their organizations as places where the diversity of Jewish voices could be expressed openly and heard. As one Avodah corps member said, "These itinerary changes would not have been possible without our collective action. We do have power in our own Jewish community . . . where diverse Jewish political identities are counted and respected."[104]

The reader may recall that it was the *intifada* in Israel that prompted Gerda Lerner to re-examine her career in terms of her Jewish identity. She concluded her article responding to the *intifada*, "A Weave of Connections," by identifying herself with an expression of Jewish universalism:

> All of us must survive in a world in which difference is the norm and no longer serves as an excuse for dominance. . . . And in order to survive in this interconnected global village we must learn and learn very quickly to respect others who are different from us and, ultimately, to grant others the autonomy we demand for ourselves.[105]

The life and career of Ruth Messinger illustrate that secular Jewish activists can be passionately motivated by the universal values inherent in the Jewish tradition to bring diverse peoples and cultures together for common mutually beneficial goals at a time when polarization and tribalism threaten to tear us apart.

Notes

1. *American Jewish World Service Reports: Judaism in Action Around the World, spring 2000.*

2. Meetings with Stan and Marcia Klein at the home of Eunice O'Hanna, Calle Nueva, San Miguel de Allende; Cave, *Messinger of Hope*, 22–25.

3. Interview with Ruth W. Messinger, October 21, 2016.

4. Ibid.

5. Cave, *Messinger of Hope*, 21.

6. Sam Roberts "Mayoral Race with a Rarity," *New York Times*, November 25, 2012; Schwarz, *Judaism and Justice*, xxi.

7. To launch the Jewish Studies Program, I organized a conference at Nassau Community College with Rabbi Michael Lerner and Professor Cornel West as lead speakers on the historical political alliances between Jews and American Blacks, a way for students to be introduced to universalist perspectives in Jewish Studies. Lerner and West had co-authored *Jews and Blacks* (see preface, Note 4). By examining positions taken on Israel by the mayoral candidates, students could also be introduced to the value of universalism as a way of moving through political conflicts toward peace.

8. Alison Mitchell, "Assassination in Israel: The New Yorkers in Israel, Pataki, Giuliani and Other Officials Remember Rabin," *New York Times*, Nov. 7, 1995.

9. Messinger qtd. in *Messinger of Hope* by Angela Cave, 24; Interview with Ruth W. Messinger, October 21, 2016.

10. Elisabeth Israels Perry, "Ruth Messinger," *Jewish Women's Archive*, https://jwa.org/encyclopedia/article/messinger-ruth.

11. Ann Haendel, a retired U.S. Federal Government administrator, served as a volunteer for the AJWS Volunteer Corps in Zimbabwe,

Senegal, Uganda, Cambodia, India, Thailand, and Kenya from 1999 to 2012.

12. Frank Bruni, "Messinger's Long Road in Pursuit of the Mayorality," *New York Times*, October 12, 1997, Section 1, Page 1.

13. Interview with Ruth W. Messinger, October 21, 2016; Perry, "Ruth Messinger," *Jewish Women's Archive*.

14. Ibid.

15. Perry, "Ruth Messinger," *Jewish Women's Archive*.

16. Interview with Ruth W. Messinger, October 21, 2016.

17. Ruth Messinger and Aaron Dorfman, "Am I My Brother's Keeper If My Brother Lives Halfway Around the World?" *Righteous Indignation: A Jewish Call for Justice*, eds. Rabbi Or N. Rose, Jo Ellen Green Kaiser, Margie Klein (Woodstock, Vermont: Jewish Lights Publishing, 2008), 281–91; and "Am I My Sibling's Keeper If My Sibling Lives Halfway Around the World?" an expanded version with textual examples, study questions, and scholarly commentaries from Jewish sources in Hebrew and English in *Walking With Justice*, eds. Rabbi Shavit Artson and Deborah Silver; United Synagogue of Conservative Judaism, the Rabbinical Assembly, Federation of Jewish Men's Clubs, Women's League for Conservative Judaism, Bel Air, California, in partnership with Zeigler School of Rabbinic Studies, American Jewish University, 2008.

18. Interview with Ruth W, Messinger, October 21, 2016.

19. Cave, *Messinger of Hope*, 8–9; Lerner, *Fireweed*, 328–34. See chapter one, Gerda Lerner, 29–30.

20. Cave, *Messinger of Hope*, 9–10.

21. Messinger, "Ruth on Chosenness" from "Bridging the Near and Far," *Sh'ma Journal*, 2015 qtd. in Cave, *Messinger of Hope*, 62.

22. See this chapter, 111–116.

23. Lerner, *Fireweed*, 337.

24. See chapter 2, Susana Wald, 65–70.

25. See preface, 65-70; Messsinger qtd. in Cave, *Messinger of Hope*, 12.

26. See Note 17.

27. Messinger and Dorfman, "Am I My Brother's Keeper If My Brother Lives Halfway Around the World?", 284–85.

28. Ibid., 283–85

29. Ibid., 285–86.
30. Cave, *Messinger of Hope*, 13–14.
31. "Black Parents Take Control, Teachers Strike Back," NPR, February 5, 2012, www.npr.org/transcripts/802593244; "Part 2: Black Parents Take Control, Teachers Strike Back," NPR, February 12, 2012, www.npr.org/transcripsts/803382499/.
32. Bruni, "Messinger's Long Road in Pursuit of the Mayorality," *New York Times*, October 12, 1997.
33. Ibid.
34. Messinger qtd. in Cave, *Messinger of Hope*, 15.
35. Ibid., italics added.
36. Cave, *Messinger for Hope*, 16-18; Messinger qtd. in *Messinger of Hope*, 19.
37. Lerner, *Fireweed*, 316.
38. Email correspondence with Messinger, July 3, 2020.
39. Rebecca Klein, "The South Isn't The Reason Schools Are Still Segregated, New York Is," Huffpost, 4/1/2016, https://www.huffpost.com/entry/new-york-school-desegregation_n_56fc7cebe4b0a06d5804bdf0; Murray I. Friedman, "The Changing Jewish Political Profile," *American Jewish History*, 91(3–4):423–438, September 2003.
40. My conversation with Jerry Siskin, a Jewish male who attended Midwood High School during the period and who spoke with a Black student about her experience being bused to Midwood High (Seminole, Florida, June 10, 2020).
41. Messinger qtd. in Cave, *Messinger of Hope*, 12.
42. Murray I. Friedman, "The Changing Jewish Political Profile." See also this chapter Note 31, and in chapter 1, Gerda Lerner, 10–11 and Notes 6 and 7.
43. Messinger, "Ruth on Civil Rights: Religious Action Center of Reform Judaism blog," August 2013 in *Messinger of Hope*, 43.
44. joachimprinz.com; "Joachim_Study_Guide.pdf," https://tjff.com/media/Joachim_Study_Guide.pdf.
45. Email correspondence with Messinger, July 3, 2020, and Ruth W. Messinger, "Bridging the Near and Far," *Sh'ma Journal*, 2015, in Cave, *Messinger of Hope*, 62.

46. Messinger, "Bridging the Near and Far" in *Messinger for Hope*, 62–63, and Cave, *Messinger for Hope*, 16.

47. *Representing Judaism: FAQs for AJWS Staff, Volunteers and In-Country Representatives*, 2nd Edition (American Jewish World Service: Pursuing Global Justice Through Grassroots Change, October 2009), 15.

48. Moss, Aron. "Are the Jews the Chosen People?" Chabad.org; https://www.chabad.org/library/article_cdo/aid/160993/jewish/ Are-the-Jews-the-Chosen-People.htm.

49. Rabbi Richard A. Hirsh, "Reconstructionist Judaism and the Rejection of the Chosen People," *My Jewish Learning*; https://www.myjewishlearning.com/article/ reconstructionist-judaism-and-the-rejection-of-chosen-people/.

50. Dr. David S. Ariel, "Chosen People: Some Modern Views," *My Jewish Learning*; https://www.myjewishlearning.com/article/ chosen-people-some-modern-views/.

51. Qtd. from Messinger, "Bridging the Near and Far" in Cave, *Messinger of Hope*, 62-63; and from Cave, *Messinger of Hope*, 16.

52. Messinger, "Bridging the Near and Far" in Cave, *Messinger of Hope*, 62.

53. Qtd. from Messinger, "Bridging the Near and Far" in Cave, *Messinger of Hope*, 62.

54. "A Conversation With Doctor Abraham Joshua Heschel," *The Eternal Light*, National Broadcasting Company under the auspices of The Jewish Theological Seminary of America, NBC/TV Network, NBC Religious Program Unit, Sunday, February 4, 1973, 2–3 p.m. EST, Interviewer Carl Stern, *NBC News*, United States Supreme Court Correspondent. Transcript of pre-recording, 2, 21.

55. Ibid., 4.

56. Ibid., 5, 9–10, 20. See also Heschel's book *The Prohpets*, cited in Note 4 of the preface.

57. "A Conversation With Doctor Abraham Joshua Heschel," *The Eternal Light*, 4.

58. Ibid., 13.

59. *Representing Judaism: FAQs for AJWS Staff, Volunteers and In-Country Representatives*, 10.

60. See chapter two, Susana Wald, 81–82.

61. See chapter one, Gerda Lerner, 14–15, 32.

62. *Representing Judaism: FAQs for AJWS Staff, Volunteers and In-Country Representatives*, 10, 15; *AJWS Reports*, Fall 2010, 19.

63. "Forward 50, 2006: Top Picks," forward.com/forward-50-2006.

64. H. Kleinon, A. Spiro, H. Krieger, "Top 50 Most Influential Jews: Places 1–10," *Jerusalem Post*, May 25, 2012, 13:49; https://www.jpost.com/jewish-world/jewish-features/top-50-mostinfluential-jews-places-1-10.

65. "Forward 50, 2006: Top Picks."

66. Cave, *Messinger of Hope*, 7.

67. Ibid., 34.

68. Ibid., 25–26.

69. Ibid., 25.

70. Ibid., 26–27; John Hagan and Wenona Rymond-Richmond, "Prologue," *Darfur and The Crime of Genocide* (New York: Cambridge University Press, 2009), xvii–xviii.

71. Cave, *Messinger of Hope*, 26–27, 46.

72. Ibid., 46–47.

73. Messinger and Dorfman, "Am I My Brother's Keeper If My Brother Lives Halfway Around the World?", 286–90.

74. Ibid., 291. Messinger and Dorfman quote Hannah Arendt, *On Revolution* (London: Penguin Books, 1963), 89.

75. Messinger and Dorfman, "Am I My Brother's Keeper If My Brother Lives Halfway Around the World?", 291–92.

76. Susan Sontag, *Regarding the Pain of Others* (New York: Picador, 2004), 102, quoted in Ruth Messinger and Aaron Dorfman, "Am I My Brother's Keeper If My Brother Lives Halfway Around the World?", 292.

77. Ruth Messinger and Aaron Dorfman, "Am I My Brother's Keeper If My Brother Lives Halfway Around the World?", 292, italics added.

78. Jacqueline DeGroot, "Jewish Philanthropy: The Concept of Tzedakah," www.learningtogive.org/resources/jewish-philanthropy-concept-tzedakah.

79. Messinger and Dorfman, "Am I My Brother's Keeper If My Brother Lives Halfway Around the World?", 292.

80. *American Jewish World Service Women's Empowerment: Global Perspectives: An AJWS High School and Adult Education Module* (New York: AJWS Education Department, 2005–2006), 2, 9–32.

81. Ibid., 11; *American Jewish World Service Annual Report 2009: Pursuing Global Justice for 25 Years: 1985–2010* (New York: AJWS, 2010), 60.

82. Ruth W. Messinger, "Reframing the Sh'ma to Repair the World", qtd. in Cave, "Ruth on Listening," *Messinger of Hope*, 53–55; JDOV Talk 2013 (Jewish Dream, Observation or Vision).

83. "Charity (Tzedakah): Eight Levels of Charitable Giving," *Jewish Virtual Library: A Project of AICE*; https://www.jewishvirtual-library.org/eight-levels-of-charitable-giving.

84. Ruth W. Messinger, "Empowerment: A Social Worker's Politics," *Practical Politics: Social Work and Political Responsibility* (National Association of Social Workers, 1982), 212–23.

85. *Representing Judaism: FAQs for AJWS Staff, Volunteers and In-Country Representatives*, 9–10.

86. Messinger, "Reframing the Sh'ma to Repair the World" qtd. in *Messinger of Hope*, 54.

87. Ibid.

88. *American Jewish World Service Women's Empowerment: Global Perspectives*, 11.

89. *American Jewish World Service Annual Report 2019: Together, We're Building a New World* (New York: AJWS, 2019), 15.

90. My interviews and exchanges with Ann Haendel took place between November and May 2020, Treasure Island, Florida.

91. See this chapter, 119–125. See also Ruth W. Messinger, "Service Is My Way of Encountering God in the World, Since God Can Only Be Found in Our Response to the Needs of Others," *I Am Jewish: Personal Reflections Inspired by the Last Words of Daniel Pearl*, 226.

92. "Meet a Donor: Questions for Rabbi Steven Leder," *AJWS Reports*, 19.

93. Ann Haendel, "The Visit," *2020 Selected Writings*, 2015.

94. See Note 79.

95. J. Correspondent, "Seniors/AJWS Phasing Out Its Volunteer Corps," *The Jewish News of Northern California* (February 1, 2013); jweekly. com/2013/02/01/seniors-ajws-phasing-out-its-volunteer-corps/.

96. Email correspondence with Messinger, July 3, 2020.

97. *American Jewish World Service Annual Report 2019: Together, We're Building a New World.*

98. Messinger, "Service Is My Way of Encountering God in the World, Since God Can Only Be Found in Our Response to the Needs of Others," *I Am Jewish: Personal Reflections Inspired by the Last Words of Daniel Pearl*, 226.

99. *Representing Judaism: FAQs for AJWS Staff, Volunteers and In-Country Representatives*, 19–20.

100. Ibid.

101. Josh Nathan-Kazis, "Israel Trip Divides Jewish Service Group," *The Forward*, November 13, 2011; https://forward.com/news/ Israel/145989/israel-trip-divides-jewish-service-group/.

102. Ibid.

103. Josh Nathan-Kazis, "Avodah Shifts Focus of Israel Trip, *The Forward*, February 23, 2012; https://forward.com/news/Israel/151839/ avodah-shifts-focus-of-israel-trip/. Shalom Hartman Institute brings a Modern Orthodox approach to dialogue with Palestinians.

104. Philip Weiss, "Jewish Social Service Groups Add a Day in Palestine to Israel Tour," *Mondoweiss*, February 24, 2012; https:// mondoweiss.net/2012/02/jewish-social-justice-groups-add-a-day-in-palestine-to-israel-tour/.

105. See chapter 1, Gerda Lerner, 33–34.

EPILOGUE

THE NEED FOR UNIVERSALISM

In the period during which I composed this book, tribalism has increased worldwide. Today, more than 70 million refugees are displaced victims of tribal conflicts and persecution in their home countries. Millions live in overcrowded camps that can hardly be called shelters without adequate nutrition, healthcare, or sanitation. Most countries in the northern hemisphere where millions of refugees seek asylum have been closed to asylum seekers due to exclusionary, ultra-nationalistic politics, another form of tribalism. Northern hemisphere, ultranationalistic ideologies target such groups as Muslims, Kurds, Central Americans, Mexicans, and Caribbeans, among others, as unwanted undesirables.[1] It is this book's contention that universal values inherent in Jewish tradition can contribute to attitudes we must develop and connections we must nurture with other cultures globally so that people of different backgrounds understand, appreciate, and respect the multiplicity of traditions we all have a human right to believe and practice. The women I have written about have embodied this hope.

Influenced by their Jewish pasts, Lerner, Wald, and Messinger, in spite of differences, have reached out as activists to marginalized human beings of non-Jewish backgrounds and sought to alleviate the ills and injustices they have suffered. It is clear the Holocaust has played a role influencing the lives of all three, two being Holocaust survivors with trauma living permanently in their consciousnesses, and one whose knowledge of the Holocaust passionately impelled her to prevent outbreaks of genocides against other peoples where witnesses stand idly by. All three women were ignited to become public and visible about their Jewish identities later in life, when conditions either allowed them safely and/or appropriately to do so, as with Lerner and Messinger, or when the oppressive politics of her nation, as in Wald's case, obligated her to speak out as a Jew. Interestingly, the mothers of all three women, to one degree or another, modeled different versions of Jewish universalism.

These three women are secular, not observant Jews. They all came to see the Exodus experience as one of the most essential messages of their Jewish identity, mandating that because Jews were strangers, they must never make strangers of others. All life is sacred; no one must be "other-ed." Acting on these beliefs as Jews, there were times when they faced questions raised in the introduction of this book: As Jews, are we obligated to devote ourselves to *tikkun olam*, the repair of the world, in the broadest global sense, or to the survival of Jewish belief and culture as embodied in Jewish institutions? Is a commitment to both possible? Does a strict adherence to fostering bonds among all peoples of the world open one to criticism for betraying or erasing one's core Jewish identity, or for impeding Jewish continuity?[2]

Global consciousness awakens us to the reality that we will not have continuity of any of our rich and varied human communities unless together we work collectively, universally, to save our planet. Under Messinger's universalist leadership, AJWS has prioritized addressing the threats posed by climate change not only by responding to world crises caused by natural disasters, but also by protecting the ecosystems and natural resources that rural and indigenous people depend on for survival.[3] In this broadest view of the Jewish obligation to repair the world, AJWS stands with other Jewish universalists like Rabbi Michael Lerner, whose writings extend the social and economic justice imperatives to include environmental justice.[4]

Messinger's example, rooting the work of AJWS in the traditions of Torah, the Prophets, the Writings, the Mishnah, and the Talmud makes it undeniable that one finds the universalist commitment to *world* improvement in the Jewish core.[5] There were times, though admittedly lasting many years, when conditions caused Messinger, Lerner, and Wald to mute their Jewish identifications because public Jewish identity would either be personally dangerous, in the cases of Lerner and Wald, or professionally inappropriate, in the case of Messinger. But never did they lose sight of who they were as Jews, and they believed—as Messinger was taught early on—that Jewish particularism exists to promote universalism.

I have come to see that the views of such secular Jews need to be more visible in a non-Jewish world that too often targets Jews for being too particular, too loyal only to one another or to Israel—right or wrong. The voices of secular, universalist Jews who believe Israelis must not deny Palestinians the same right to self-determination that they themselves possess must not be silenced. This view is clearly expressed by Gerda Lerner.[6]

I have come to see that the universal, ethical values running through Judaism that are held and carried by secular Jews, and a growing number of observant Jews, need to be more widely emphasized and known if we hope to reach the goal of world peace.[7]

Notes

1. *Hias Haggadah: Welcome the Stranger, Protect the Refugee*, https://www.hias.org/passover; United Nations, "Refugees," un.org/en/sections/issues-depth/refugees/.

2. See introduction, 1–2.

3. *American Jewish World Service Annual Report 2009*, 10–14, 30, 33 and *American Jewish World Service Annual Report* 2019, 6, 18–21.

4. Rabbi Michael Lerner's newest book, *Revolutionary Love: A Political Manifesto to Heal and Transform the World*, is a comprehensive proposal for "a fundamental change in consciousness in ourselves and in every part of national and global society . . . to prevent the destruction of the life support system of Earth . . . and to achieve lasting global peace."

5. See chapter 3, Note 47. *Representing Judaism: FAQs for AJWS Staff, Volunteers and In-Country Representatives* summarizes the Jewish sources underlying the work of AJWS, 9–16. Also see chapter 3, Note 17: Messinger and Dorfman, "Am I My Brother's Keeper If My Brother Lives Halfway Around the World?"

6. See chapter 1, Gerda Lerner, 33–34.

7. See preface, Note 3. Observant Jews serving in the Shalom Hartman Institute have written about universal values in Judaism that help them overcome their conflict with Palestinians—for example, Yossi Klein Halevi's *Letters to My Palestinian Neighbor* (New York: Harper-Perennial, 2019). Young Hasidic Jews in Crown Heights, Brooklyn, where violent riots broke out in 1991 over Black/Jewish conflict, have demonstrated in support of Black Lives Matter. Emily Wax-Thibideau, "Young Hasidic Jews Protest in Support of Black Neighbors, Challenging History of Racial Tensions," *Washington Post*, June 19, 2020; https://www.washingtonpost.com/national/young-hasidic-jews-challenge-history-of-community-tensions-with-protest-in-support-of-black-neighbors/2020/06/19/e16aea56-abdf-11ea-a9d9-a81c1a491c52_story.html: "The opposite of love is not hate. It's indifference, one sign read, quoting Holocaust survivor and Nobel Peace laureate Elie Wiesel. The young families chanted 'Black lives matter!' and 'Jews for justice!' as they marched through the diverse neighborhood, once home to riots that broke out over tensions between black and Hasidic residents."

ACKNOWLEDGMENTS

T he ideas for this book originally developed in Rosh Chodesh gatherings of the Am HaYam Cape Cod Havurah from 2007–10 when our topic was our Jewish journeys. Many of us had left Jewish observance early in our lives, but felt connected to Jewish identity and wanted to explore the nature of that connection more fully as adults in our later years. I am grateful to Bernice Simon-Wolfson for organizing Rosh Chodesh, and for her willingness, as well as Cheryl Dockser's, to be interviewed by me on the theme of reconnecting with Jewish identity. I give thanks also to Jewish women in the Mexican communities of San Miguel de Allende and Oaxaca—Miranda Nadel and Susana Wald, respectively—who also allowed me to interview them on the same theme.

Even earlier, in the 1990s, Ann Davis in Poughkeepsie, New York, organized a feminist Jewish women's study group to which I belonged in order to rediscover women's role in Jewish history. When I decided in 2013 to develop the project of turning points in adult women's return to Jewish connection, I interviewed Ann Davis as well. I thank Ann Davis for her interview and for her early leadership researching the new feminist Jewish scholarship. I thank the Northeast Feminist Scholars (MF1)—to which Ann and I belonged, along with Tucker Farley, Julie Matthaei, Nan Wiegersma, Rachael Kamel, and Sue Rouda—for providing the intellectual context for placing religious studies among movements for social change.

I am grateful also to Rabbi Michael Lerner and Cat Zavis for continuing a progressive, Jewish vision of a compassionate world free of inequity and injustice in both *Tikkun* Magazine and the Network of Spiritual Progressives. Their work illustrates the ongoing relevance of

Jewish Studies to the psychological, economic, political, and environmental problems plaguing people and the planet today.

I am grateful to my writing coach Kathleen Spivack, who brought the unusual Jewish arc of women's historian Gerda Lerner to my attention, knowing I was teaching from Gerda Lerner's writing in my Women's Studies classes. I thank Kathleen Spivack as well for reading drafts of my book, and for suggesting I add to each chapter my personal associations with the three women who are the subjects of this study—Gerda Lerner, Susana Wald, and Ruth W. Messinger.

I am also deeply grateful to Susana Wald, who became a personal friend and writing buddy during the years I spent in Oaxaca, for her encouragement with this book. My heartfelt gratitude extends to Ruth W. Messinger, whose political career I admired but whom I only came to know personally once her career with American Jewish World Service was coming to a close. She, like Susana Wald, spent many hours with me being interviewed, reading and rereading drafts, and corresponding.

I thank Holocaust and genocide scholar Robert Melson for reading drafts of this manuscript and offering excellent suggestions for revision. I owe great thanks also to Ann Haendel, who shared information with me from her personal library and conversed with me about her many years' experience volunteering with American Jewish World Service.

I am grateful to Judi Sitkin for reading early drafts of the developing manuscript, offering valuable suggestions, and beginning work on indexing, all with encouraging words. I thank Kahren Dowcett, who read later chapters and offered important comments about the perspective of non-Jewish readers.

I thank the serious fellow and sister writers in Brewster Writers for urging me forward and helping me sharpen the focus and meaning of this book over several years. I thank sister writer Tonia St. Germain for leading the group at various junctures and for showing me unlimited bounds of support.

I owe special, heartfelt thanks to my brother Ron Leder for his unflagging technological assistance and professional formatting of my manuscript, and to my devoted sister Devorah Vidal for her loving patience with my questions about Jewish orthodoxy.

I add my gratitude to Claudia Volkman for the care and thoroughness of her outstanding copyediting. I am grateful to Karen Strauss, publisher of Hybrid Global Publishing, for excellent professional guidance. Thank you also Sara Foley at Hybrid Global for ushering the publication process from start to finish.

Thanks go to Larry Baker for his final index and bibliography.

For my own reconnection with a Jewish past that I had put on a shelf, I am grateful to Milton Teichman, my husband and life partner, who asked me to collaborate on projects dealing with literature on the Holocaust. That intimate and caring collaboration led to my full immersion in Jewish history and texts.

SELECTED BIBLIOGRAPHY

Adler, Margot. "Inner Space: The Spiritual Frontier." *feminist.com*, 2003. www.feminist.com/resources/artspeech/insp/inner.html.

Allmer, Patricia. *Angels of Anarchy: Women Artists and Surrealism*. Prestel Publishing, 2009.

———. "Feminist Interventions: Revising the Canon." In *A Companion to Dada and Surrealism*, edited by David Hopkins, 366–81. John Wiley & Sons, 2016.

American Jewish World Service Annual Report 2009: Pursuing Global Justice for 25 Years: 1985–2010. American Jewish World Service, 2010.

American Jewish World Service Annual Report 2019: Together, We're Building a New World. American Jewish World Service, 2019.

American Jewish World Service Reports: Judaism in Action Around the World, spring 2000.

American Jewish World Service Women's Empowerment: Global Perspectives: An AJWS High School and Adult Education Module. AJWS Education Department, 2005–2006.

Antler, Joyce. "History and Gender." *Frontiers: A Journal of Women's Studies* 36, no. 1 (2015): 16–21.

———. *Jewish Radical Feminism: Voices from the Women's Liberation Movement*. New York University Press, 2018.

———. "Remembering Gerda Lerner: The 'Mother' of Women's History." *Jewish Women's Archive*, January 13, 2013. https://jwa.org/blog/remembering-gerda-lerner-mother-of-womens-history.

Arendt, Hannah. *The Human Condition*. University of Chicago Press, 1958.

———. *On Revolution*. Penguin Books, 1963.

Ariel, David S. "Chosen People: Some Modern Views." *My Jewish Learning.* https://www.myjewishlearning.com/article/chosen-people-some-modern-views/.

Arnott, Joanne. "Susana Wald: Voyage to the Bottom," February 1, 2013. joannearnott.blogspot.com/2013/02/Susana-wald-voyage-to-the-bottom.html

Barer, Deborah. "Between Public and Private: Navigating the Jewishness of Hannah Arendt." academia.edu/1689003/Between_Public_and_Private_Navigating_the_Jewishness_of_Hannah_Arendt.

"Black Parents Take Control, Teachers Strike Back." NPR, February 5, 2012. www.npr.org/transcripts/802593244; "Part 2: Black Parents Take Control, Teachers Strike Back." NPR, February 12, 2012, www.npr.org/transcripsts/803382499/.

Bracey, John H., Jr. "Afro-American Women: A Brief Guide to Writings from Historical and Feminist Perspectives." *Contributions in Black Studies: A Journal of African and Afro-American Studies* 8, no. 9 (1986). http://scholarworks.umass.edu/cibs/vol8/iss1/9.

Bravo-Cox, Macarena. Master's degree on feminist Surrealist artists at Écoles des Hautes Etudes en Sciences Sociales. Artes y Lenguajes, mención Estética, Paris, France, 2015–17.

———. "Susana Wald: The Woman of Herself" ("Susana Wald: La mujer de símisma"), Agulha Revista de Cultura 1999–2020, Arc Edições/Uma Agulha em todo o mundo, August 26, 2019.

Breton, André. *Manifesto of Surrealism,* 1924. https://www.tcf.ua.edu/Classes/Jbutler/T340/SurManifesto/ManifestoOfSurrealism.htm.

Breton, André, and Diego Rivera. "Manifesto for a Revolutionary Independent Art, 1938." *Marxist Literary Criticism,* 2001. https://www.marxists.org/subject/art/lit_crit/works/rivera/manifesto.htm. (It is believed Breton wrote the Manifesto with Leon Trotsky, although it was signed by Diego Rivera.)

Broner, E.M. *The Telling: The Story of a Group of Jewish Women Who Journey to Spirituality through Community and Ceremony.* Harper, 1993.

Brown, Michael. "Biography: Henrietta Szold 1860–1945." *Jewish Women's Archive.* https://jwa.org/article/biography-henrietta-szold-1860-1945.

Brownmiller, Susan. *Against Our Will.* Simon and Schuster, 1975.

Bruni, Frank. "Messinger's Long Road in Pursuit of the Mayorality." *New York Times*, October 12, 1997, Section 1, Page 1.

Cave, Angela. *Messinger of Hope: A Portrait of Ruth W. Messinger.* American Jewish World Service, 2016.

"Charity (Tzedakah): Eight Levels of Charitable Giving." *Jewish Virtual Library: A Project of AICE.* https://www.jewishvirtuallibrary.org/eight-levels-of-charitable-giving.

"Chile Buries General as Martyr." *New York Times Archive*, October 27, 1970. https://www.nytimes.com/1970/10/27/archives/chile-buries-general-as-martyr.html.

Chowers, Eyal. "The Late Blooming Vision of Henrietta Szold," *Dissent,* March 29, 2012. dissentmagazine.org/onlinearticles/the_late_blooming_vision_of_henrietta_szold.

Claybourne, Anna. *Surrealism.* Heinemann Library, 2009.

Compton, Sophia. "Evolution of an Archetype: Emergence of the Feminine Shekinah." In *The Transcendent Feminine: Shekinah Glory, From Theophany to Theosophy,* by Madonna S. Compton. CreateSpace Independent Publishing Platform, 2013. *Academia*, 1–18, https://www.academia.edu/29077353/Evolution_of_an_Archetype_Emergence_of_the_Feminine_Shekinah.

Conley, Katharine. "Review of *Surrealism and the Politics of Eros, 1938–1968.*" *French Forum* 31, no.3 (Fall 2006): 168–70.

"A Conversation with Doctor Abraham Joshua Heschel." *The Eternal Light.* National Broadcasting Company under the auspices of the Jewish Theological Seminary of America, NBC/TV Network, NBC Religious Program Unit, Sunday, February 4, 1973, 2–3 p.m. EST, Interviewer Carl Stern, *NBC News*, United States Supreme Court Correspondent. Transcript of pre-recording, 2, 21.

Correa-Cabrera, Guadalupe. "Political Factionalism in Southern Mexico: The Case of Oaxaca 2006." *Journal of Politics in Latin America* 4, no. 1 (January 2012): 93–96.

Crenshaw, Kimberlé. "Demarginalizing the Intersection of Race and Sex: A Black Feminist Critique of Antidiscrimination Doctrine, Feminist Theory, and Antiracist Politics." *University of Chicago Legal Forum*, issue 1 (1989): 139–67.

De Shong Meador, Betty. *Inanna, Lady of the Largest Heart*. University of Texas Press, 2001.

DeGroot, Jacqueline. "Jewish Philanthropy: The Concept of Tzedakah." *Learning to Give*. www.learningtogive.org/resources/jewish-philanthropy-concept-tzedakah.

Denham, Diana, and C.A.S.A. Collective, eds. *Teaching Rebellion: Stories from the Grassroots Mobilization in Oaxaca*. PM Press, 2008.

The Eugenio Granell Foundation. http://www.eugeniogranell.org/eugenio-granell.

Firestone, Shulamit. *The Dialectics of Sex*. William Morrow & Co., 1970.

Firestone, Tirzah. *With Roots in Heaven: One Woman's Passionate Journey into the Heart of Her Faith*. Dutton, 1998.

"Forward 50, 2006: Top Picks," forward.com/forward-50-2006.

Friedman, Murray I. "The Changing Jewish Political Profile." *American Jewish History* 91, no. 3–4 (September 2003):423–38.

Ghiuzeli, Haim F. "Crypto-Jews in Mexico during Spanish Colonial Era." *Museum of the Jewish People at Beit Hatfutsot*. https://www.bh.org.il/visit-us/general-information/.

Green, David. B. "This Day in Jewish History/Hungary Enacts First Jewish Law." *Haaretz*, May 29, 2014. https://www.haaretz.com/jewish/.premium-this-day-hungary-enacts-first-anti-jewish-law-1.5250019.

Hagan, John, and Wenona Rymond-Richmond. *Darfur and the Crime of Genocide*. Cambridge University Press, 2009.

Halevi, Yossi Klein. *Letters to My Palestinian Neighbor*. Harper-Perennial, 2019.

Hartman, Donniel. *Putting God Second: How to Save Religion from Itself*. Beacon Press, 2016.

Heschel, Abraham Joshua. *The Insecurity of Freedom: Essays on Human Experience*. Schocken Books, 1972.

———.*The Prophets*. Harper and Row, 1962.

HIAS Haggadah: Welcome the Stranger, Protect the Refugee. HIAS. https://www.hias.org/passover.

Higgins, Charlotte. "Leonora Carrington: Wild at Heart." *The Guardian*, January 25, 2015. https://www.theguardian.com/artanddesign/2015/jan/28/leonara-carrington-wild-at-heart.

Hirsh, Rabbi Richard A. "Reconstructionist Judaism and the Rejection of the Chosen People." *My Jewish Learning.* https://www.myjewishlearning.com/article/reconstructionist-judaism-and-the-rejection-of-chosen-people/.

History.com editors. "Chilean President Salvador Allende Dies in Coup." *History,* July 23, 2020. https://www.history.com/this-day-in-history/allende-dies-in-coup.

"Hungarian Labor Service Battalions." *Geni.* https://www.geni.com/projects/Hungarian-Labor-Service-Battalions/14800.

Hungary in the Soviet Orbit." *Encyclopedia Britannica.* https://www.britannica.com/place/Hungary/Hungary-in-the-Soviet-orbit.

"Hungary-Postwar Hungary." http://countrystudies.us/hungary/36.htm.

International Military Trial at Nuremburg. https://www.ushmm.org/wlc/en/article.php?ModuleId=10005201.

Jackson, Livia Bitton. "Somarja: March 28, 1944." In *I Have Lived a Thousand Years: Growing Up in the Holocaust*, 30. Simon and Schuster, 1997.

Kaplan, Mordecai. *Judaism as a Civilization: Towards a Reconstruction of American-Jewish Life.* Jewish Publication Society, 2010.

Kaye-Kantrowitz, Melanie. "To Be a Radical Jew in the Late 20th Century." In *The Tribe of Dina: A Jewish Women's Anthology,* edited by Melanie Kaye-Kantrowitz and Irena Klepfisz, 297–320.Sinister Wisdom Books, 1986.

Klein, Rebecca. "The South Isn't the Reason Schools Are Still Segregated, New York Is." Huffpost, April 1, 2016. https://www.huffpost.com/entry/new-york-school-desegregation_n_56fc7cebe4b0a06d5804bdf0.

Kleinon, H., A. Spiro, and H. Krieger, "Top 50 Most Influential Jews: Places 1–10," *Jerusalem Post,* May 25, 2012. https://www.jpost.com/jewish-world/jewish-features/top-50-most-influential-jews-places-1-10.

Klimó, Árpád von. *Remembering Cold Days: The 1942 Massacre of Novi Sad, Hungarian Politics and Society 1942–1989.* University of Pittsburgh Press, 2018.

Leder, Sharon, and Teichman, Milton, eds. *The Burdens of History: Post-Holocaust Generations in Dialogue.* Merion Westfield Press International, 2000.

Lerner, Gerda. *Black Women in White America*. Pantheon, 1972.

———. "The Covenant." In *The Creation of Patriarchy*, 188–93. Oxford University Press, 1986.

———. *The Creation of Feminist Consciousness*. Oxford University Press, 1993.

———. *Fireweed: A Political Autobiography*. Temple University Press, 2002.

———. *The Grimké Sisters of South Carolina*. Houghton Mifflin, 1967.

———. "The Lady and the Mill Girl." *American Studies Journal* 10, no. 1 (spring 1969): 5–15.

———. *The Majority Finds Its Past*. Oxford University Press, 1979.

———. *Why History Matters*. Oxford University Press, 1997.

Lerner, Michael. *The Left Hand of God: Taking Back Our Country from the Religious Right*. Harper Collins, 2006.

———. *Revolutionary Love: A Political Manifesto to Heal and Transform the World*. University of California Press, 2019.

Lerner, Michael, and Cornel West. *Jews and Blacks: A Dialogue on Race, Religion, and Culture in America*. Plume, 1996.

Li, Melody. "UConn Professor Emeritus Recalls March on Washington." UConn, Neag School of Education, November 7, 2013. https://education.uconn.edu/2013/11/07/uconn-professor-emeritus-recalls-march-on-washington/.

Liska, Manuela, and Vivian Liska. *Sartre, Jews, and the Other: Rethinking Antisemitism, Race, and Gender*. De Gruyter Oldenbourg, 2020.

Lowenthal, Marvin. *Henrietta Szold: Life and Letters*. Viking Press, 1942.

Lyons, John Joseph. "Aldo Pellegrini: The Subversive Effect of Poetry." *Johnjosephlyons*. https://johnjosephlyons.com/2020/03/31/aldo-pellegrini-the-subversive-effect-of-poetry/.

Mabey, Martha. "Susana Wald." In *Susana Wald: Celebration*, by Susana Wald, 16–29. El colegio de Oaxaca, 2003.

Manatakis, Lexi. "Seven Female Artists Who Subverted Surrealism." *Dazed*, April 2019. https://www.dazeddigital.com/art-photography/article/43833/1/seven-female-artists-who-subverted-surrealism-dorothea-tanning-tate-modern.

"Meet A Donor: Questions for Rabbi Steven Leder." *AJWS Reports*, Fall 2010, 19.

Messinger, Ruth W. "Empowerment: A Social Worker's Politics." In *Practical Politics: Social Work and Political Responsibility*, edited by Maryann Mahaffey, 212–23.National Association of Social Workers, 1982.

————. "Service Is My Way of Encountering God in the World, Since God Can Only Be Found in Our Response to the Needs of Others." In *I Am Jewish: Personal Reflections Inspired by the Last Words of Daniel Pearl*, edited by Judea Pearl and Ruth Pearl, 225-226. Jewish Lights Publishing, 2004.

Messinger, Ruth W., and Aaron Dorfman. "Am I My Brother's Keeper if My Brother Lives Halfway around the World?" In *Righteous Indignation: A Jewish Call for Justice*, edited by Rabbi Or N. Rose, Jo Ellen Green Kaiser, and Margie Klein, 281–91. Jewish Lights Publishing, 2008.

————. "Am I My Sibling's Keeper if My Sibling Lives Halfway Around the World?" In *Walking with Justice*, edited by Rabbi Shavit Artson and Deborah Silver; United Synagogue of Conservative Judaism, the Rabbinical Assembly, Federation of Jewish Men's Clubs, Women's League for Conservative Judaism, Bel Air, California, in partnership with Ziegler School of Rabbinic Studies. American Jewish University, 2008.

"Mexico." World Jewish Congress (WJC). https://www.worldjewishcongress.org/en/about/communities/MX.

Meyer, David. "Anti-Semitism in Europe: Jews Are Outsiders, Not Equals." *Haaretz*, March 3, 2013. https://www.haaretz.com/opinion/.premium-david-meyer-jews-still-on-european-fringe-1.5232403.

Millet, Kate. *Sexual Politics*. Columbia University Press, 1969.

Mitchell, Alison. "Assassination in Israel: The New Yorkers in Israel, Pataki, Giuliani and Other Officials Remember Rabin." *New York Times*, November 7, 1995.

Moss, Aron. "Are the Jews the Chosen People?" *Chabad.org*. https://www.chabad.org/library/article_cdo/aid/160993/jewish/Are-the-Jews-the-Chosen-People.htm.

Nathan-Kazis, Josh. "Avodah Shifts Focus of Israel Trip. *The Forward*, February 23, 2012. https://forward.com/news/Israel/151839/avodah-shifts-focus-of-israel-trip/.

————."Israel Trip Divides Jewish Service Group." *The Forward*, November 13, 2011. https://forward.com/news/Israel/145989/israel-trip-divides-jewish-service-group/.

Neumann, Erich. *The Great Mother: Analysis of the Archetype*, translated by Ralph Manheim. Princeton University Press, 1955.

"New York City Teachers' Strike of 1968; Blacks and Jews Battle over Control of Black School District." Originalpeople.org. https://originalpeople.org/new-york-city-teachers-strike-of-1968-blacks-and-jews-battle-over-control-of-black-school-district/.

Nicholson, Melanie. *Surrealism in Latin American Literature: Searching for Breton's Ghost*. Palgrave Macmillan, 2013.

Nikolic, Ivana. "Last Survivors Recall WWII Massacre in Occupied Yugoslavia." *Balkan Transitional Justice*, January 23, 2019. https://balkaninsight.com/2019/01/23/last-survivors-recall-wwii-massacre-in-occupied-yugoslavia-01-22-2019/.

Novitski, Joseph. "Allende, Marxist Leader, Elected Chile's President." *New York Times Archive*, October 25, 1970. https://www.nytimes.com/1970/10/25/archives/allende-marxist-leader-elected-chiles-president-allende-elected.html.

Oisteanu, Andrei. *Inventing the Jew: Antisemitic Stereotypes in Romania and Other Central-East European Cultures*. University of Nebraska-Press, 2009.

Owens, Lance S. "C.J. Jung and Erich Neumann: The Zaddik, Sophia and the Shekinah." *Psychological Perspectives: A Quarterly Journal of Jungian Thought* 61, no. 2 (2018). https://www.academia.edu/31768301/C._G._Jung_and_Erich_Neumann_The_Zaddik_Sophia_and_the_Shekinah_2016_2018_.

Parsons, Talcott. *The Social System*. Routledge and Kegan Paul, 1951.

Perdigó, Luisa M. *The Origins of Vicente Huidobro's 'Creacionismo' (1911–1916) and Its Evolution (1917–1947)*. Mellen, 1994.

Perry, Elisabeth Israels. "Ruth Messinger." *Jewish Women's Archive*. https://jwa.org/encyclopedia/article/messinger-ruth.

Plaskow, Judith. *Standing Again at Sinai: Judaism from a Feminist Perspective*. Harper, 1990.

Podair, Jerald E. *The Strike That Changed New York: Blacks, Whites, and the Ocean Hill-Brownsville Crisis*. Yale University Press, 2002.

Power, Susan L. "Surrealist Intrusion and Disenchantment on Madison Avenue, 1960." In *Networking Surrealism in the USA: Agents, Artists, and the Market,* by Julia Drost, Fabrice Flahutez, Anne Helmreich, and Martin Schieder, 428–47. Heidelberg arthstoricum.net, 2019. https://books.ub.uni-heidelberg.de/arthistoricum/reader/download/485/485-17-87215-1-10-20191209.pdf.

"Raoul Wallenberg: Rescue of Hungarian Jews." *Jewish Virtual Library: A Project of AICE.* jewishvirtuallibrary.org/raoul-wallenberg-2.

"Raoul Wallenberg and the Rescue of Jews in Budapest," *United States Holocaust Memorial Museum Holocaust Encyclopedia.*encyclopedia.ushmm.org/content/en/article/raoul-wallenberg-and-the-rescue-of-jews-in-budapest.

"Refugees." United Nations. un.org/en/sections/issues-depth/refugees/.

Representing Judaism: FAQs for AJWS Staff, Volunteers and In-Country Representatives. 2nd ed. American Jewish World Service: Pursuing Global Justice through Grassroots Change, October 2009.

Roberts, Sam. "Mayoral Race with a Rarity." *New York Times,* November 25, 2012.

Rockaway, Robert. "Introduction: The Jew as 'Other' in America." *Jewish History* 89, no. 4 (December 2001): 353–545.

Rozett, Robert. "Conscripted Slaves: Hungarian Jewish Forced Laborers on the Eastern Front during World War II." *Yad Vashem.* https://www.yadvashem.org/articles/general/conscripted-slaves-hungarian-jewish-forced-laborers.html.

Sanderson, Brenton. "Tristan Tzara and the Jewish Roots of Dada, Part 1." *Occidental Observer,* November 15, 2011. www.theoccidentalobserver.net/2011/11/15/tristan-tzara-and-the-jewish-roots-of-dada-part-1/.

Schneider, Susan Weidman. *Jewish and Female: A Guide and Sourcebook for Today's Jewish Woman.* Touchstone, 1985.

Schnier, Jacques. "Erich Neumann, The Great Mother: An Analysis of the Archetype." *College Art Journal* 16, no. 1 (1956): 78–80. https://www.tandfonline.com/doi/abs/10.1080/15436322.1956.11466169?journalCode=rcaj19

Schultz, Debra L. *Going South: Jewish Women in the Civil Rights Movement.* New York University Press, 2001.

Schwarz, Sidney. *Judaism and Justice: The Jewish Passion to Repair the World*. Jewish Lights, 2006.

Short, Robert S. "The Politics of Surrealism 1920–36." *Journal of Contemporary History* 1, no. 2: 3–25. https://www.jstor.org/stable/259920?seq=1.

Sontag, Susan. *Regarding the Pain of Others*. Picador, 2004.

Stan Shaw Collection. https://archives.qc.cuny.edu/finding_aids/.

Starkman, Alvin, and Arlene Starkman. "Not a Jew to Be Found?" *Casa Machaya, Oaxaca Bed and Breakfast*. http://www.oaxacadream.com/articles/academic4.html.

Starkman, Susan, compiler. *Joachim Prinz: I Shall Not Be Silent*. Toronto Jewish Film Festival; Ontario Trillium Foundation; Cineplex. joachimprinz.com; "Joachim_Study_Guide.pdf," https://tjff.com/media/Joachim_Study_Guide.pdf.

Teichman, Milton, and Sharon Leder, eds. *Truth and Lamentation: Stories and Poems on the Holocaust*. University of Illinois Press, 1998.

"This Day in History, February 8, 1949, Cardinal Mindszenty of Hungary Sentenced." *History*. https://www.history.com/this-day-in-history/cardinal-mindszenty-of-hungary-sentenced.

Van Raay, Stefan, Joanna Moorhead, and Teresa Arcq. *Surreal Friends: Leonora Carrington, Remedios Varo and Kati Horna*. Lund Humphries, 2010.

Vorspan, Albert, and David Saperstein. *Jewish Dimensions of Social Justice: Tough Moral Choices of Our Time*. URJ Press, 1998.

Wald, Susana. *Daily Spanish for Dummies: Mini Edition*. Wiley Publishing, 2010.

———. *Life Matters: Windows*. Unpublished memoir (2013–17).

———. *Spanish for Dummies*. Berlitz and IDG Books, 1999.

———. *Spanish Phrases for Dummies*. Wiley Publishing, 2004.

———. *Susana Wald: Celebration*. El colegio de Oaxaca, *2003*.

———. *Tres grandes poemas de Enjeduena dedicados a Inanna*. UACM, Difusión Cultural y Extensión Universitaria, 2009.

Wallace, Ruth A., and Alison Wolff. *Contemporary Sociological Theory: Continuing the Classical Tradition*. 4th ed. Prentice Hall, 1995.

Watson, Alice Rethinger. "The Life and 'Crimes' of Cardinal Mindszenty." *Catholic Culture*. https://www.catholicculture.org/culture/library/view.cfm?recnum=661.

Wax-Thibideau, Emily. "Young Hasidic Jews Protest in Support of Black Neighbors, Challenging History of Racial Tensions." *Washington Post*, June 19, 2020. https://www.washingtonpost.com/national/young-hasidic-jews-challenge-history-of-community-tensions-with-protest-in-support-of-black-neighbors/2020/06/19/e16aea56-abdf-11ea-a9d9-a81c1a491c52_story.html.

Weiss, Philip. "Jewish Social Service Groups Add a Day in Palestine to Israel Tour." *Mondoweiss*, February 24, 2012. https://mondoweiss.net/2012/02/jewish-social-justice-groups-add-a-day-in-palestine-to-israel-tour/.

Wiesel, Elie. *Night.* Hill and Wang, 1960.

Willis, Bruce Dean. *Aesthetics of Equilibrium: The Vanguard Poetics of Vicente Huidobro and Mário de Andrade.* Purdue University Press, 2006.

Wolfe, Robert. "From Habiru to Hebrew: The Roots of the Jewish Tradition." *New English Review,* October 2009. http://www.new-englishreview.org/Robert_Wolfe/From_Habiru_to_Hebrews%3A_The_Roots_of_the_Jewish_Tradition/.

Yanklowitz,Shmuly. *The Soul of Jewish Social Justice.* Urim Publications, 2014.

Zeller, Ludwig. "Afterword by the Author." In *To Saw the Beloved Only When Necessary.* Translated into English by Susana Wald, Beatriz Zeller, A.F. Moritz, and Robin Skelton, 101. Exile Editions, 1990.

———.*The Rules of the Game: Selected Shorter Poems 1952–2008,*translated by A. F. Moritz. Quattro Books, 2012.

INDEX